A Guide to
The National Hunt Pattern

This book, a companion volume to 'A Guide to the
Pattern: The Top Races of the Flat Season', is a race-
by-race guide to all the events of which the National
Hunt Pattern is comprised, with conditions of entry
and details of past results. The introduction and
commentaries have been provided by George Rae, a
racing correspondent of *The Times* and author of 'The
Sporting Life Guide to Owning a Racehorse'.

A Guide to
THE NATIONAL HUNT
PATTERN

The top races of the Jumps Season

With introduction and commentaries by George Rae

The Sporting Life
in association with
The Jockey Club

Cover picture
The 1992 Victor Chandler Chase (Ascot 2m): Young Snugfit (left)
and Waterloo Boy (Photo: *The Sporting Life*)

Photo credits
Text illustrations are *Sporting Life* photographs

Acknowledgements
The author expresses thanks to all those who have helped in the
compilation of this volume, in particular to Ruth Quinn of the Race
Planning Department of The Jockey Club

Published by The Sporting Life
Orbit House, 1 New Fetter Lane, London EC4A 1AR
in association with
The Jockey Club, 42 Portman Square, London W1H 0EN

First edition 1992

ISBN 0 901091 44 8

Text typeset by LBJ Enterprises Ltd, Chilcompton and Aldermaston
Cover origination by Reprosharp Ltd, London EC1
Text printed and bound by The Bath Press, Bath
Cover printed by Ark Litho, London SW19

Contents

Preface

Any new publication requires its own set of guidelines and this, the first 'Guide to the National Hunt Pattern', is no exception.

As the book deals with races of differing status, the Grade 1 contests, the summit of the Pattern, have been made immediately identifiable by including ten years of past results while the races in Grades 2 and 3 have five.

An endlessly changing sport makes particular demands. The sponsors quoted in the race titles are the latest available. Where the race is known to be without a sponsor at the time of going to press, the name of the race alone has been used.

Nor are race conditions immune to change. Where penalties are involved in handicap races, the date from which penalties can be incurred will sometimes change from the one quoted, but only by a matter of days. Once the date for the publication of the weights has been set, the penalty date will always be the Saturday before.

Every effort has been made to make the information carried here as up-to-date as possible, but anyone considering entering a horse in a National Hunt Pattern race is advised to confirm the conditions in the *Racing Calendar*, the official publication of the Jockey Club.

The 1992 Scottish Champion Hurdle (Ayr 2m): Granville Again winning from Jinxy Jack (middle) and Fidway

8

Introduction

At the heart of the National Hunt Pattern lies a simple objective: to encourage competitive top-level racing which is attractive to the public.

The pattern race system is not simply a dusty theory to be argued over in committee rooms. It must be about horses and racing, in particular about providing opportunities to bring the best horses together on the track. That, of course, does not happen by accident. By definition, the word Pattern describes order and method, a planned framework. Add to that a desire to cultivate quality and the twin pillars on which the Pattern stands can be identified: a framework which provides a series of opportunities for the best horses of all ages over a range of distances.

Once the commitment has been made to quality and competition, it follows that the Pattern must be selective. To include too many races defeats the object of the exercise. The merit of a Pattern race win is devalued, not least because the best horses have ever greater opportunities to avoid each other. To be a champion, a horse has to beat the best around. Nor should it be forgotten that every follower of racing, no matter how casual or enthusiastic, has as great a stake in the Pattern as owners and trainers. He gains from the excitement of the best in competition, and just as surely loses when lack of opportunity drives champions into minor events in which no-one will oppose them.

This book concerns the National Hunt Pattern and comparisons with the Flat Pattern will be kept to a minimum. However, one fundamental difference is worth dispensing with here. Flat racing is significantly more international than National Hunt racing and that is reflected in the Flat Pattern, which is structured to cover the major European racing countries. The National Hunt Pattern concerns only Britain. Although runners do move between Britain, Ireland and France, it is a limited traffic. Each country might occasionally cast an eye towards the others, but primarily each will look after its own affairs.

This, then, is the development of that Pattern. It has grown beyond all recognition since its earliest days almost thirty years ago, reaching a sophistication its founding fathers would scarcely have believed. Remember, too, that the Pattern is a constantly changing creature. It has evolved through the years to meet the demands of an endlessly developing sport and, when circumstances demand, will continue to do so.

The origin of the Pattern

National Hunt racing at its highest level was first recognised in 1964 with a grant of £20,000, called a Prestige race allocation, from the Horseracing Betting Levy Board. The allocation was divided between three races, the Grand National, which received £10,000, and the Cheltenham Gold Cup and the Champion Hurdle, each of which received £5,000.

With the principle of recognising top-class jump racing established, the following year the Levy Board allotted £70,000 to Feature races although the amount given to the three Prestige races was unchanged. Racecourses were given financial help, depending on each course's status, to promote their own Feature race.

During the period 1966-69, the Prestige race allocation remained unchanged but the amount given to Feature races more than doubled to £144,500. It was during this time, in 1968, that the Jump Race Planning Committee was established under the chairmanship of Lord Leverhulme. The recommendations of the Committee led to the creation of a recognisable form of National Hunt Pattern from which today's structure has evolved.

The Levy Board allocated £40,000 to the infant Pattern, in addition to its contributions to the Prestige and Feature Race programmes. The first Jump Pattern, in 1969, encompassed 14 races, with steeplechasing having numerical and financial priority.

The first Pattern

Hurdles	Allocation
Fighting Fifth (Newcastle)	£5,000
Big Ben (Ascot)	£2,500
Free Handicap (Chepstow)	£2,500
Berkshire (Newbury)	£2,500
Northern (Haydock)	£2,500
Total	£15,000

Steeplechases	Allocation
National Hunt Two-Mile Champion (Cheltenham)	£5,000

Grange (Ascot)	£2,500
Welsh Grand National (Chepstow)	£2,500
Coventry (Kempton)	£2,500
Beech (Sandown)	£2,500
Scottish Grand National (Ayr)	£2,500
Sandown Pattern (Sandown)	£2,500
Wetherby Pattern (Wetherby)	£2,500
Doncaster Pattern (Doncaster)	£2,500
Total	£25,000

In 1971 the Pattern race allocation was increased to £60,000 but the Feature race allocation was dropped and the money distributed to courses via other avenues. Over the next decade the Pattern grew substantially and in 1974 the Jump Race Pattern Committee was established.

The growth of the Pattern

Year	Allocation	Year	Allocation
1971	£60,000	1982	£351,000
1972	£60,000	1983	£311,500
1973	£60,000	1984	£311,500
1974	£93,250	1985	£311,500
1975	£108,250	1986	£311,500
1976	£148,250	1987	£311,500
1977	£163,250	1988	£327,100
1978	£230,000	1989	£387,000
1979	£253,000	1990	£497,000
1980	£276,000	1991	£695,000
1981	£311,000	1992	£505,000

Note: The increased 1991 figure reflects additional Levy Board support to launch the restructured National Hunt Pattern. The 1992 figure, a 27.5 per cent cut, stemmed from reduced levy income during a recession. The allocation for 1993 is going to be £675,000.

The objective of the Jump Pattern underwent a fundamental change with the Holland-Martin Review in 1982. Until then, the Jump Pattern had been a collection of important and successful races considered worthy of additional prize-money. It had no single wider brief, unlike the more established Flat Pattern, which provided a series of races for individual categories of horse stretching throughout the season.

Although the Jump Pattern grew during the Seventies it lacked a single objective. Races were afforded Pattern status by the Jump

11

Pattern Race Committee, who considered annually requests from racecourses wishing to promote particular races. The Committee was not looking for these races to fill a pre-determined slot in the calendar, but awarded Pattern status by the criteria that the race in question consistently attracted top-class runners and did not detract from an existing Pattern race. Impartiality towards tracks also loomed large in the Committee's thinking. In one season, Pattern races were run on 21 different courses, illustrating the desire to encourage as many racecourses as possible, no matter how small, to promote important races.

The Holland-Martin Committee was set up to investigate the success of the Jump Pattern. Its first, and most important impression, was that the Pattern had no clearly defined objective. Certainly Pattern races were benefiting from the Levy Board's financial assistance, but the Committee was concerned that the spread of races provided too many opportunities for top-class horses to avoid each other.

Also, the growth in the number of Pattern races was diluting the available prize-money among too many Pattern events. With those points at the top of its agenda, the Holland-Martin Committee included among its recommendations:

• To encourage top horses to run against each other, the number of Pattern races should be reduced from 81 to 45 and Pattern race values significantly increased.

• Although the number of Pattern races would be reduced, three Listed races – the English, Scottish and Welsh Grand Nationals should receive Pattern-style grants.

• Pattern races should be run evenly through the main part of the season, but not before mid-October or after the end of April.

• Pattern races should be run on Saturdays with television coverage to maximise their exposure.

• The Pattern race programme should cover nine categories:

Hurdles	Chases
Juveniles	2m Novices
2m Novices	2½m Novices
2½m Novices	2-2½m Open
2m Open	3m Open
2½m+ Open	

• Pattern races should be classified into two grades. Grade 1 to include championship races, Grade 2 to cover races just below Grade 1 status and include selected conditions races and limited handicaps.

After the restructured Pattern had been in place for three seasons a further review was undertaken but no fundamental changes were made. However, in 1989, the National Hunt Pattern was completely overhauled. A review group, appointed by the Race Planning Committee of the Jockey Club, proceeded with the following brief:

> To provide the supreme spectacle of competitive racing over fences and hurdles for the best horses divided by age, experience and distance. The opportunities to be spaced throughout the season to ensure a programme of continuity, with prize-money being commensurate with the importance of the race.

The objective of the Pattern, therefore, was confirmed as the creation of a comprehensive structure which, to a large extent, should ensure that the best horses need not run outside it. The key to the re-working of the Pattern was the decision that the season should have two peaks, the first around Christmas/New Year, the second based around the Cheltenham and Aintree festivals.

It was seen as a flaw in the previous Pattern that it revolved almost exclusively around Cheltenham, which, while the showpiece of National Hunt racing, put all the eggs in one basket. Should a horse miss his engagement at Cheltenham, for whatever reason, then connections lost their one and only championship opportunity.

But identifying the season's two peaks was only part of the problem. To know one's destination is one thing, but just as important is having the means to get there. The Pattern needed to provide two stepping stones – lead-up races – to each championship race, with, after Cheltenham or Aintree, a consolation race for the various distance groups.

From such requirements, the framework of the Pattern evolved:

Hurdles	Categories	
Juvenile	Lead-up race	(Grade 2)
2m novice	Lead-up race	(Grade 2)
2m 4f novice	Championship race	(Grade 1)
2m open hurdle	Lead-up race	(Grade 2)
2m 4f open hurdle	Lead-up race	(Grade 2)
3m open hurdle	Championship race	(Grade 1)
	Consolation race	(Grade 2)

Chases	Categories	
2m novice	Lead-up race	(Grade 2)
2m 4f novice	Lead-up race	(Grade 2)
3m novice	Championship race	(Grade 1)
2m open chase	Lead-up race	(Grade 2)
2m 4f open chase	Lead-up race	(Grade 2)
3m open chase	Championship race	(Grade 1)
	Consolation race	(Grade 2)

Thus, the framework of the Pattern comprised 12 race groups with 7 categories of race in each group. Multiplying the two produced a Pattern of 84 races. Additionally, three specific races, the Gerry Feilden Hurdle at Newbury, the H & T Walker Handicap Chase at Ascot and the Belle Epoque Sefton Novices' Hurdle at Aintree, would be incorporated into the Pattern at Grade 2 status.

The terminology of the Pattern was also reviewed, races being classified as Grade 1, Grade 2 and Grade 3, similar to the Flat Pattern's usage of Groups 1, 2 and 3, rather than such imprecise terms 'Championship', 'Feature' and 'Listed' employed under the previous Pattern. With a numerical classification, the standing of any particular race would be readily identifiable.

Major handicaps were also to have a part to play in the Pattern. To many in the industry, and to the public, the top handicaps are glamour events, generating wide interest, in-depth media coverage and, not least, as highly competitive events, producing sizeable levy turnover through betting. Inclusion, however, has been highly selective. Just 14 races – 8 chases and 6 hurdles – have been added to the Pattern with Grade 3 status.

The newly-constituted Pattern thus comprises 101 races, to be run throughout the country. To summarise:

Grade 1	24	North	31
Grade 2	63	Midlands	26
Grade 3	14	South	44
Total	101	Total	101

List of National Hunt Pattern races

Note: Sponsorship details subject to change

Date	Race	Grade	Racecourse
October	Desert Orchid South Western Pattern Chase	2	Wincanton
November	Charlie Hall Chase	2	Wetherby
November	West Yorkshire Hurdle	2	Wetherby
November	Wensleydale Juvenile Hurdle	2	Wetherby
November	Plymouth Gin Haldon Gold Cup Chase	2	Devon & Exeter
November	Mackeson Gold Cup Handicap Chase	3	Cheltenham
November	Aga Worcester Novices' Chase	2	Worcester
November	Racecall Ascot Hurdle	2	Ascot
November	Hurst Park Novices' Chase	2	Ascot
November	H & T Walker Gold Cup Handicap Chase	2	Ascot
November	Kennel Gate Castle Novices' Hurdle	2	Ascot
November	Hennessy Cognac Gold Cup Handicap Chase	3	Newbury
November	Newbury Long Distance Hurdle	2	Newbury
November	Gerry Feilden Hurdle	2	Newbury
November	Bellway Homes 'Fighting Fifth' Hurdle	2	Newbury
November	Clive Lewis Classic Novices' Hurdle	2	Uttoxeter
November	Peterborough Chase	2	Huntingdon
November	Crowngap Winter Novices' Hurdle	2	Sandown
December	William Hill Handicap Hurdle	3	Sandown
December	Mitsubishi Shogun Tingle Creek Handicap Chase	2	Sandown
December	Henry VIII Novices' Chase	2	Sandown
December	Rehearsal Handicap Chase	2	Chepstow
December	Bula Hurdle	2	Cheltenham
December	A F Budge Novices' Hurdle	2	Cheltenham
December	A F Budge Gold Cup Handicap Chase	3	Cheltenham
December	Summit Junior Hurdle	2	Lingfield
December	Lowndes Lambert December Novices' Chase	2	Lingfield
December	Kilroe Group Waterloo Hurdle	2	Haydock
December	Youngmans Long Walk Hurdle	1	Ascot
December	Rovacabin Noel Novices' Chase	2	Ascot
December	Coral Welsh National (Handicap Chase)	3	Chepstow
December	Finale Junior Hurdle	1	Chepstow
December	King George VI Chase	1	Kempton
December	Feltham Novices' Chase	1	Kempton
December	Top Rank Christmas Hurdle	1	Kempton
December	Castleford Chase	1	Wetherby
December	Northumberland Gold Cup (Novices' Chase)	1	Newcastle
December	Challow Novices' Hurdle	1	Newbury
January	Newton Chase	1	Haydock
January	Baring Securities Tolworth Novices' Hurdle	1	Sandown
January	PML Lightning Novices' Chase	2	Ascot
January	Victor Chandler Handicap Chase	2	Ascot
January	Dipper Novices' Chase	2	Newcastle
January	Peter Marsh Handicap Chase	2	Haydock
January	Jim Ennis Construction Premier Long Distance Hurdle	2	Haydock
January	FK Roofing Champion Hurdle Trial	2	Haydock
January	Rossington Main Novices' Hurdle	2	Doncaster
January	River Don Novices' Hurdle	2	Doncaster
January	Bishops Cleeve Hurdle	1	Cheltenham
January	Food Brokers Finesse Four-Year-Old Hurdle	2	Cheltenham
January	West of Scotland Pattern Novices' Chase	2	Ayr
February	Tote Jackpot Handicap Hurdle	3	Sandown
February	Agfa Diamond Handicap Chase	2	Sandown
February	Scilly Isles Novices' Chase	1	Sandown
February	Marston Moor Handicap Chase	2	Wetherby
February	Reynoldstown Novices' Chase	2	Ascot
February	Tote Gold Trophy Handicap Hurdle	3	Newbury
February	Game Spirit Chase	2	Newbury
February	Persian War Premier Novices' Hurdle	2	Chepstow
February	Nottinghamshire Novices' Chase	2	Nottingham

List continues on p.16

February	Regency Hurdle	2	Warwick
February	Kingwell Hurdle	2	Wincanton
February	Racing Post Handicap Chase	3	Kempton
February	Rendlesham Hurdle	2	Kempton
February	Tote Placepot Hurdle	2	Kempton
February	Mitsubishi Shogun Galloway Braes Novices' Chase	2	Kempton
February	Dovecote Novices' Hurdle	2	Kempton
February	Westminster-Motor Taxi Insurance Cavalier Chase	2	Worcester
March	Berkshire Hurdle	2	Newbury
March	Smurfit Champion Hurdle Challenge Trophy	1	Cheltenham
March	Bonusprint Stayers' Hurdle	1	Cheltenham
March	Waterford Castle Arkle Challenge Trophy	1	Cheltenham
March	Trafalgar House Supreme Novices' Hurdle	1	Cheltenham
March	Queen Mother Champion Chase	1	Cheltenham
March	Sun Alliance Novices' Chase	1	Cheltenham
March	Sun Alliance Novices' Hurdle	1	Cheltenham
March	Tote Cheltenham Gold Cup	1	Cheltenham
March	Daily Express Triumph Hurdle	1	Cheltenham
March	County Handicap Hurdle	3	Cheltenham
March	Northern Trust Opal Novices' Chase	2	Lingfield
March	Letheby & Christopher Long Distance Hurdle	2	Ascot
April	Seagram Top Novices' Hurdle	2	Aintree
April	Sandeman Maghull Novices' Chase	2	Aintree
April	Martell Cup Chase	2	Aintree
April	Glenlivet Anniversary 4-Y-O Hurdle	2	Aintree
April	Mumm Melling Chase	1	Aintree
April	Mumm Mildmay Novices' Chase	2	Aintree
April	Heidsieck Dry Monopole Novices' Hurdle	2	Aintree
April	Martell Aintree Hurdle	1	Aintree
April	Martell Aintree Handicap Chase	2	Aintree
April	Martell Grand National (Handicap Chase)	3	Aintree
April	Janneau Mersey Novices' Hurdle	2	Aintree
April	Scottish Champion Hurdle	2	Ayr
April	William Hill Scottish National (Handicap Chase)	2	Ayr
April	Edinburgh Woollen Mills Future Champion Novices' Chase	1	Ayr
April	EBF Novices' Hurdle Final (Handicap)	3	Cheltenham
April	South Wales Showers Silver Trophy Chase	2	Cheltenham
April	Whitbread Gold Cup (Handicap Chase)	3	Sandown
May	St Modwen Staffordshire Hurdle	2	Uttoxeter
May	Swinton Handicap Hurdle	3	Haydock
May	Godiva Kingmaker Novices' Chase	2	Warwick

Late revision: Heidsieck Dry Monopole Novices' Hurdle (Aintree, April)
now Belle Epoque Sefton Novices' Hurdle

Juvenile hurdles

In National Hunt terms, a juvenile hurdler is a three-year-old in the first part of the season and a four-year-old after New Year's Day, when all horses celebrate their birthday. It is as a three-year-old that a horse is first allowed to run under National Hunt rules.

It remains one of the great paradoxes of the jumping season that a group whose most obvious traits are, by definition, inexperience and immaturity should contest one of the year's most demanding races, the Daily Express Triumph Hurdle at the Cheltenham Festival. The race invariably draws a big field, is almost always run at a strong gallop from start to finish and, more often than not, produces a surprise result (not since Attivo in 1974 has the favourite won).

It is noticeable that in recent seasons more and more lightly-raced horses are contesting the Triumph Hurdle, which has tended to mean that horses prominent in the early season races have been overtaken as the season progresses. In the 1992 Triumph, for example, 22 of the 30 overnight acceptors had not run more than four times, and many of those had been contesting relatively minor races at the smaller tracks.

Duke Of Monmouth, the 1992 winner, was having only his fourth race, while other similar recent winners include Kribensis, Alone Success and First Bout, all successful on only their third start. Some, however, do keep going strongly throughout the season, none better than the gallant Royal Derbi. During the 1988-89 season he ran no fewer than 15 races in Britain and Ireland, collecting the Wensleydale Juvenile Hurdle at Wetherby in the autumn – the first of the category's lead-up races – adding the Tote Placepot Hurdle at Kempton Park in February before finishing a creditable fourth to Ikdam in the Triumph.

South Parade is an example of a horse who showed much his best form in the first part of the season. In the 1987-88 season he won the Summit Hurdle at Lingfield Park and then the Finale Hurdle at Chepstow, usually a highly competitive race, both numerically and in terms of quality. He could, however, do no better than fourth in his five subsequent starts that season.

Curiously, despite the fact that it usually produces a decent horse, the winners of the Finale Hurdle have a poor record in the Triumph, perhaps a further illustration of the divide between the early- and late-season horses. Oh So Risky did bridge the gap by winning a Pattern race in the first half of the season, the Summit Hurdle, on the way to taking the Triumph, but it has to be said that he is in the minority.

Wensleydale Hurdle
(Grade 2, Wetherby, early November)
for three yrs old only
about TWO MILES

Weights: 10st 12lb each
Fillies allowed 5lb
Penalties, a winner of a hurdle race value £2000 . . . . .4lb
Of a hurdle race, or hurdle races collectively value £5000 . . . . .8lb

	Winner	Trainer	Jockey	SP	Ran
1987	Royal Illusion, 3-10-7	G Moore	K Mooney	7/1	17
1988	Royal Derbi, 3-10-11	N Callaghan	W Humphreys	7/2	25
1989	Native Friend, 3-11-1	J Fitzgerald	M Dwyer	4/1	14
1990	Native Mission, 3-10-12	J Fitzgerald	M Dwyer	4/1	10
1991	Swift Sword, 3-10–12	Mrs G Reveley	P Niven	11/8f	9

Summit Hurdle
(Grade 2, Lingfield Park, early December)
for three yrs old only
TWO MILES ABOUT HALF A FURLONG

Weights: 10st 12lb each

Fillies allowed 5lb
Penalties, a winner of a hurdle race value £2500 . . . . .4lb
Of a hurdle race value £4000 . . . . .7lb

	Winner	Trainer	Jockey	SP	Ran
1987	South Parade, 3-11-0	G Balding	G Bradley	11/4f	15
1988	Take Issue, 3-11-0	J Sutcliffe	Dale McKeown	20/1	15
1989	not run, due to construction of all-weather track				
1990	Oh So Risky, 3-10-12	D Elsworth	P Holley	4/5f	10
1991	None So Brave, 3-11-2	R Akehurst	J Osborne	4/6f	7

Finale Hurdle
(Grade 1, Chepstow, late December)
for three yrs old only
TWO MILES ABOUT HALF A FURLONG

Weights: 11st each

Fillies allowed 5lb

	Winner	Trainer	Jockey	SP	Ran
1982	Primrolla, 3-11-0	D Nicholson	H Davies	3/1	14
1983	Dodgy Future, 3-11-0	S Mellor	M Perrett	2/1	14
1984	Out Of The Gloom, 3-11-0	R Hollinshead	J J O'Neill	7/1	13
1985	The Footman, 3-11-0	D Elsworth	G Bradley	11/1	12
1986	High Knowl, 3-11-0	M Pipe	P Scudamore	4/5f	9
1987	South Parade, 3-11-3	G Balding	G Bradley	15/8f	7
1988	Enemy Action, 3-11-3	M Pipe	P Scudamore	8-15f	9
1989	Crystal Heights, 3-11-0	Mrs J Retter	B Powell	33-1	10
1990	Hopscotch, 3-10-9	M Pipe	J Lower	9/4f	13
1991	Good Profile, 3-11-0	G Moore	L Wyer	7/1	18

Food Brokers Finesse Hurdle
(Grade 2, Cheltenham, late January)
for four yrs old only
TWO MILES ABOUT ONE FURLONG

Weights: 11st each

Fillies allowed 5lb
Penalties, a winner of a hurdle race value £3000 . . . . .4lb
Of a hurdle race value £6000 . . . . .8lb

	Winner	Trainer	Jockey	SP	Ran
1988	Jason's Quest, 4-11-0	J Baker	M Williams	16/1	9
1989	Highland Bud, 4-11-3	D Nicholson	R Dunwoody	4/1	6
1990	Sayyure, 4-11-8	N Tinkler	G McCourt	3/1	4
1991	Hopscotch, 4-11-2	M Pipe	P Scudamore	8/11f	7
1992	abandoned, frost				

Tote Placepot Hurdle
(Grade 2, Kempton Park, late February)
for four yrs old only
about TWO MILES

Weights: 10st 12lb each

Fillies allowed 5lb
Penalties, a winner of a hurdle race value £3000 . . . . .4lb
Of a hurdle race value £6000 . . . . .8lb

	Winner	Trainer	Jockey	SP	Ran
1988	Russian Affair, 4-11-0	R Akehurst	Dale McKeown	7/1	12
1989	Royal Derbi, 4-11-3	N Callaghan	H Davies	10/1	6
1990	Philosophos, 4-11-0	J Baker	W McFarland	33/1	11
1991	Marlingford, 4-10-12	Mrs J Jordan	D Morris	20/1	7
1992	Qualitair Sound, 4-10-12	J Bottomley	J J Quinn	11/1	8

Daily Express Triumph Hurdle
(Grade 1, Cheltenham, mid-March)
for four yrs old only
TWO MILES ABOUT ONE FURLONG

Weights: 11st each

Fillies allowed 5lb

	Winner	Trainer	Jockey	SP	Ran
1983	Saxon Farm, 4-11-0	S Mellor	M Perrett	12/1	30
1984	Northern Game, 4-11-0	E O'Grady (Ire)	T J Ryan	20/1	30
1985	First Bout, 4-11-0	N Henderson	S Smith Eccles	5/1	27
1986	Solar Cloud, 4-11-0	D Nicholson	P Scudamore	40/1	28
1987	Alone Success, 4-11-0	N Henderson	S Smith Eccles	11/1	29
1988	Kribensis, 4-11-0	M Stoute	R Dunwoody	6/1	26
1989	Ikdam, 4-11-0	R Holder	N Coleman	66/1	27
1990	Rare Holiday, 4-11-0	D Weld (Ire)	B Sheridan	25/1	30
1991	Oh So Risky, 4-11-0	D Elsworth	P Holley	14/1	27
1992	Duke Of Monmouth, 4-11-0	S Sherwood	M Richards	33/1	30

Glenlivet Anniversary 4-y-o Hurdle
(Grade 2, Aintree, early April)
for four yrs old only
TWO MILES ABOUT HALF A FURLONG

Weights: 11st each

Fillies allowed 5lb
Penalties, a winner of a hurdle race value £15000 . . . . .4lb

	Winner	Trainer	Jockey	SP	Ran
1988	Royal Illusion, 4-11-0	G Moore	M Hammond	9/1	14
1989	Vayrua, 4-11-0	G Harwood	M Perrett	12/1	9
1990	Sybillin, 4-11-0	J Fitzgerald	D Byrne	25/1	18
1991	Montpelier Lad, 4-11-0	G Richards	N Doughty	9/1	14
1992	Salwan, 4-11-0	P Bevan	R Stronge	5/1jf	13

Two-mile novice hurdles

The winner of the Trafalgar House Supreme Novices' Hurdle, the second of the category's championship races, can be guaranteed a certain fame. Its duration is uncertain but it can be estimated at not less than 35 minutes.

The Supreme Novices' Hurdle opens the Cheltenham Festival and so provides its first talking point. As talking points go, there will be few bigger than the victory of Destriero in 1991. His owner, Noel Furlong, landed a simply monumental coup, which he then proceeded to play up, unsuccessfully, on The Illiad in the Champion Hurdle.

Furlong certainly had Destriero's measure. The second and third that day were Granville Again and Gran Alba, both high-class novices who were to go on to land important wins the following season. Destriero's win also underlined the difficulty of building a Pattern for novice hurdlers. He came to Cheltenham with just one race, and one win, behind him, a path which was followed by his successor, Flown, in 1992.

The majority of the last ten winners of the race have been brought along relatively quietly, winning mostly unspectacular races outside the Pattern. Vagador was an interesting exception, however, preceding his Cheltenham win with a victory against proven handicappers in the National Spirit Challenge Trophy at Fontwell Park.

The category does seem to split into distinct sections, with those prominent in the early lead-up races, and indeed the first championship race, the Tolworth Hurdle at Sandown Park, often overtaken by those whose day comes in the latter part of the season.

It is interesting that the Tolworth Hurdle, while certainly producing its share of good horses, seems to have diverted its winners away from the apparently natural objective of the Supreme Hurdle at Cheltenham.

Of the last ten winners, eight have run at Cheltenham but only three, Away We Go, Forest Sun and New York Rainbow, in the Supreme Novices. The progression surely cannot be that harmful as Forest Sun won and both Away We Go and New York Rainbow ran a creditable fourth. Of the remaining five, two (Desert Orchid and Wishlon) contested the Champion Hurdle, Midnight Count the Stayers' Hurdle, Wing And A Prayer the Triumph Hurdle, and

Change The Act the Sun Alliance Novices' Hurdle over two-and-a-half miles.

The consolation race, the Seagram 100 Pipers Top Novices' Hurdle at Aintree, has been strongly contested lately. Carobee, an exciting talent, had Flown behind him when winning in 1992, while his predecessors include Granville Again, who beat Gran Alba in 1991, and the talented if sometimes erratic Fidway who won the previous year.

Kennel Gate Castle Novices' Hurdle
(Grade 2, Ascot, mid-November)
for four yrs old and upwards which, at the start of the current season, have not won a hurdle race
TWO MILES ABOUT HALF A FURLONG

Weights: 11st each

Fillies and mares allowed 5lb
Penalties, a winner of a hurdle race value £2500 . . . . .4lb
Of a hurdle race value £4000 . . . . .7lb

	Winner	Trainer	Jockey	SP	Ran
1987	Away We Go, 5-11-6	J Jenkins	S Sherwood	15/8	10
1988	Lalitpour, 4-11-1	J Jenkins	S Sherwood	9/2	6
1989	Arden, 5-11-5	C Brooks	P Scudamore	5/6f	8
1990	Gaasid, 5-11-0	R Akehurst	L Harvey	6/4f	7
1991	abandoned, fog				

A F Budge Novices' Hurdle
(Grade 2, Cheltenham, early December)
for four yrs old and upwards which, at the start of the
current season, have not won a hurdle race
TWO MILES ABOUT ONE FURLONG

Weights: 11st each

Fillies and mares allowed 5lb
Penalties, a winner of a hurdle race value £2500 . . . . .4lb
Of a hurdle race value £4000 . . . . .7lb

	Winner	Trainer	Jockey	SP	Ran
1987	Butt And Ben, 3-11-0	F Walwyn	R Chapman	12/1	5
1988	Green Willow, 6-11-3	J Gifford	Peter Hobbs	7/1	18
1989	Run For Free, 5-11-0	M Pipe	P Scudamore	9/4jf	6
1990	abandoned, snow				
1991	Thetford Forest, 4-11-0	D Nicholson	R Dunwoody	5/4f	6

Baring Securities Tolworth Novices' Hurdle
(Grade 1, Sandown Park, early January)
for four yrs old and upwards which, at the start of the
current season, have not won a hurdle race
TWO MILES ABOUT HALF A FURLONG

Weights: 4-y-o . . . . 10st 9lb; 5-y-o and up 11st 7lb
Fillies and mares allowed 5lb

	Winner	Trainer	Jockey	SP	Ran
1983	Hawksbarrow, 5-11-5	D Gandolfo	P Barton	13/2	4
1984	Desert Orchid, 5-11-11	D Elsworth	C Brown	5/6f	6
1985	Wing And A Prayer, 4-10-13	J Jenkins	J Francome	5/4f	6
1986	Midnight Count, 6-11-7	J Gifford	R Rowe	9/4	7
1987	Mister Point, 5-11-7	C Tinkler	G McCourt	5/1	9
1988	Away We Go, 6-11-11	J Jenkins	S Smith Eccles	4/6f	11
1989	Wishlon, 6-12-0	R Smyth	I Shoemark	4/6f	4
1990	Forest Sun, 5-11-12	G Balding	J Frost	8/11f	7
1991	Change The Act, 6-11-7	O Sherwood	J Osborne	9/1	6
1992	New York Rainbow, 7-11-7	N Henderson	J Kavanagh	5/1	7

Rossington Main Novices' Hurdle
(Grade 2, Doncaster, late January)
for four yrs old and upwards which, at the start of the
current season, have not won a hurdle race
TWO MILES ABOUT HALF A FURLONG

Weights: 4-y-o . . . . 10st 7lb; 5-y-o and up 11st 5lb
Fillies and mares allowed 5lb
Penalties, a winner of a hurdle race value £3000 . . . . .4lb
Of a hurdle race value £6000 . . . . .7lb

	Winner	Trainer	Jockey	SP	Ran
1988	Drumlin Hill, 5-11-0	F Winter	P Scudamore	15/2	9
1989	Cruising Altitude, 6-11-7	O Sherwood	S Sherwood	5/4f	5
1990	Peanuts Pet, 5-11-0	B McMahon	T Wall	4/5f	6
1991	Ruling, 5-11-0	R Johnson-Houghton	P Niven	11/8f	7
1992	abandoned, frost				

Dovecote Novices' Hurdle
(Grade 2, Kempton Park, late February)
for four yrs old and upwards which, at the start of the
current season, have not won a hurdle race
about TWO MILES

Weights: 4-y-o . . . . 10st 7lb; 5-y-o and up 11st 3lb
Fillies and mares allowed 5lb
Penalties, a winner of a hurdle race value £3000 . . . . .4lb
Of 2 such races, or of one value £6000 . . . . .7lb

	Winner	Trainer	Jockey	SP	Ran
1988	Over The Winter, 6-10-11	N Henderson	J Osborne	7/2	14
1989	Decided, 6-11-9	O Sherwood	S Sherwood	8/1	12
1990	Stratford Ponds, 5-11-1	O Sherwood	J Osborne	4/1	19
1991	Granville Again, 5-11-3	M Pipe	P Scudamore	11/4	14
1992	Flown, 5-11-3	N Henderson	R Dunwoody	3/1	5

25

Trafalgar House Supreme Novices' Hurdle
(Grade 1, Cheltenham, mid-March)
for four yrs old and upwards which, at the start of the
current season, have not won a hurdle race
TWO MILES ABOUT HALF A FURLONG

Weights: 4-y-o . . . . .11st; 5-y-o and up 11st 8lb
Fillies and mares allowed 5lb

	Winner	Trainer	Jockey	SP	Ran
1983	Buck House, 5-11-8	M Morris (Ire)	T Carmody	8/1	22
1984	Browne's Gazette, 6-11-8	M Dickinson	Mr D Browne	11/2	18
1985	Harry Hastings, 6-11-8	J S Wilson	C Grant	14/1	30
1986	River Ceiriog, 5-11-8	N Henderson	S Smith-Eccles	40/1	29
1987	Tartan Tailor, 6-11-8	G Richards	P Tuck	14/1	20
1988	Vagador, 5-11-8	G Harwood	M Perrett	4/1f	26
1989	Sondrio, 8-11-8	M Pipe	J Lower	25/1	21
1990	Forest Sun, 5-11-8	G Balding	J Frost	7/4f	18
1991	Destriero, 5-11-8	A Geraghty (Ire)	P McWilliams	6/1	21
1992	Flown, 5-11-8	N Henderson	J Osborne	13/2	17

Seagram Top Novices' Hurdle
(Grade 2, Aintree, early April)
for four yrs old and upwards which, at the start of the
current season, have not won a hurdle race
TWO MILES ABOUT HALF A FURLONG

Weights: 4-y-o . . . . .10st 10lb; 5-y-o and up 11st 2lb
Fillies and mares allowed 5lb
Penalties, a winner of a hurdle race value £4000 . . . . .4lb
Of a hurdle race value £10000 . . . . .8lb

	Winner	Trainer	Jockey	SP	Ran
1988	Faraway Lad, 5-11-0	O Sherwood	S Sherwood	10/1	14
1989	Young Benz, 5-11-0	M H Easterby	L Wyer	3/1f	11
1990	Fidway, 5-11-0	T Thomson Jones	S Smith Eccles	16/1	15
1991	Granville Again, 5-11-6	M Pipe	P Scudamore	5/4f	8
1992	Carobee, 5-11-10	D Nicholson	R Dunwoody	2/1	9

Two-and-a-half mile novice hurdles

If ever a horse could be said to have championed a particular section of the Pattern it would have been Slalom underlining the merits of the two-and-a-half mile novice hurdles division. Slalom ran in seven races during the 1987-88 season, five of them now in this section of the Pattern. Indeed, if his defeat when favourite for the Tote Jackpot Handicap Hurdle at Sandown Park is included, he stepped outside the Pattern only for his seasonal debut, in a novice hurdle at Kempton Park.

After that Kempton race, he won the Reynoldstown Novices Hurdle, the Crowngap Winter Hurdle at Sandown Park and the Challow Hurdle at Newbury, respectively two lead-up races and the first championship event. Later came the Persian War Hurdle at Chepstow, in which he finished third to Sir Blake, and the Sun Alliance Novices' Hurdle at the Cheltenham Festival, where he was beaten only by a head by Rebel Song.

But that level of continuity has generally been much harder to find. In common with the two-mile novice hurdle category, the staying novices of recent years have been more lightly raced. Of the last ten Sun Alliance winners, six had not run more than four times.

Interestingly, though, the last two, Crystal Spirit and Thetford Forest, made their respective ways to Cheltenham via other areas of the Pattern. Crystal Spirit prefaced his Festival win with a high-class victory over more experienced opponents in the Bishops Cleeve Hurdle, also at Cheltenham, the first championship race in the two-and-a-half mile open hurdle division. Little wonder he started as low as 2/1 favourite in a field of 29 for the Sun Alliance.

Thetford Forest stayed among the novices, but showed good form over two miles when taking the A F Budge Hurdle at Cheltenham in December. Thetford Forest's win did, however, highlight one trend. Like previous winners Rebel Song and Sayfar's Lad, he won the Boddingtons Bitter Novices' Trial Hurdle at Warwick in February. Although the race is outside the Pattern, it has gained a reputation as a solid trial for the Sun Alliance.

The consolation race, the Janneau Mersey Novices' Hurdle at

Aintree, has been well contested. Sir Blake and Morley Street both ran in the Sun Alliance before their victories, while Crystal Spirit's attempt at the double was denied by Shannon Glen. In fact, the quality of the race can be seen from the fact that among recent runners-up have been no less than Blazing Walker, Trapper John and Remittance Man.

The 1992-93 season will see a change in this division. The Reynoldstown Novices' Hurdle will be replaced by an equivalent race at Uttoxeter, the Clive Lewis Classic Novices' Hurdle, although the new race will aim to attract precisely the same type of horse. For that reason, a certain licence has been employed in attributing the results of the Reynoldstown to the infant Uttoxeter race.

Clive Lewis Classic Novices' Hurdle
(Grade 2, Uttoxeter, mid-November)
for four yrs old and upwards which, at the start of the current season, have not won a hurdle race
TWO MILES ABOUT FOUR AND A HALF FURLONGS

Weights: 11st each

Fillies and mares allowed 5lb
Penalties, a winner of a hurdle race value £2500 . . . . .4lb
Of a hurdle race value £4000 . . . . .7lb

Results for Reynoldstown Novices' Hurdle at Wolverhampton

	Winner	Trainer	Jockey	SP	Ran
1987	Slalom, 6-10-12	M Robinson	J White	9/4f	13
1988	abandoned, frost				
1989	Tajroba, 4-11-2	J Jenkins	R Dunwoody	100/30	8
1990	Tyrone Bridge, 4-11-0	M Pipe	R Dunwoody	1/2f	5
1991	Bollin Patrick, 6-11-0	M H Easterby	R Garritty	13/8f	7

Crowngap Winter Novices' Hurdle

(Grade 2, Sandown Park, early December)
for four yrs old and upwards which, at the start of the
current season, have not won a hurdle race
TWO MILES ABOUT SIX FURLONGS

Weights: 11st each

Fillies and mares allowed 5lb
Penalties, a winner of a hurdle race value £2500 . . . . .4lb
Of a hurdle race value £4000 . . . . .7lb

	Winner	Trainer	Jockey	SP	Ran
1987	Slalom, 6-11-6	M Robinson	J White	6/4f	9
1988	Man On The Line, 5-11-6	R Akehurst	P Scudamore	4/7f	10
1989	abandoned, frost				
1990	Tyrone Bridge, 4-11-7	M Pipe	R Dunwoody	1/5f	4
1991	Arabian Sultan, 4-11-0	M Pipe	P Scudamore	7/4f	8

Challow Hurdle

(Grade 1, Newbury, late December/early January)
for three yrs old and upwards which, at the start of the
current season, have not won a hurdle race
TWO MILES ABOUT FIVE FURLONGS

Weights: 3-y-o . . . . 10st 7lb; 4-y-o and up 11st 8lb
Fillies and mares allowed 5lb

	Winner	Trainer	Jockey	SP	Ran
1983	Ambiance, 4-10-12	P Bailey	P Scudamore	7/4	3
1983*	Catch Phrase, 5-11-5	J Gifford	P Double	11/4f	8
1984	The Breener, 5-11-5	O Sherwood	S Sherwood	15/8f	9
1985	abandoned, frost				
1987	Bonanza Boy, 6-11-12	P Hobbs	Peter Hobbs	4/1	8
1988	Slalom, 7-11-12	M Robinson	J White	8/11f	4
1988†	Green Willow, 6-11-13	J Gifford	Peter Hobbs	13/8	4
1989	Forest Sun, 4-11-13	G Balding	J Frost	6/4f	8
1990	Tyrone Bridge, 4-11-8	M Pipe	R Dunwoody	2/5f	4
1991	Lift And Load, 4-11-8	R Hannon	G McCourt	5/4f	6

* 31 December   † 30 December

The 1991 Sun Alliance Hurdle (Cheltenham 2m 5f): Crystal Spirit leads Minorettes Girl

River Don Novices' Hurdle
(Grade 2, Doncaster, late January)
for four yrs old and upwards which, at the start of the
current season, have not won a hurdle race
TWO MILES ABOUT FOUR FURLONGS

Weights: 4-y-o .... 10st 7lb; 5-y-o and up 11st 6lb
Fillies and mares allowed 5lb
Penalties, a winner of a hurdle race value £3000 .... 4lb
Of a hurdle race value £6000 .... 7lb

	Winner	Trainer	Jockey	SP	Ran
1991	Cab On Target, 5-11-4	Mrs G Reveley	P Niven	10/11f	7
1992	abandoned, frost				

Persian War Premier Novices' Hurdle
(Grade 2, Chepstow, mid-February)
for four yrs old and upwards which, at the start of the
current season, have not won a hurdle race
TWO MILES ABOUT FOUR AND A HALF FURLONGS

Weights: 4-y-o .... 10st 10lb; 5-y-o and up 11st 7lb
Fillies and mares allowed 5lb
Penalties, a winner of a hurdle race value £3000 .... 3lb
Of a hurdle race value £6000 .... 6lb

	Winner	Trainer	Jockey	SP	Ran
1988	Sir Blake, 7-11-10	D Elsworth	C Brown	10/1	8
1989	abandoned, waterlogged				
1990	abandoned, waterlogged				
1991	abandoned, snow				
1992	Mighty Mogul, 5-11-7	Mrs J Pitman	M Pitman	11/8f	6

Sun Alliance Novices' Hurdle
(Grade 1, Cheltenham, mid-March)
for four yrs old and upwards which, at the start of the
current season, have not won a hurdle race
TWO MILES ABOUT FIVE FURLONGS

Weights: 4-y-o . . . . .10st 12lb; 5-y-o and up 11st 7lb
Fillies and mares allowed 5lb

	Winner	Trainer	Jockey	SP	Ran
1983	Sabin Du Loir, 4-10-8	M Dickinson	G Bradley	16/1	27
1984	Fealty, 4-10-12	P Brookshaw	S J O'Neill	33/1	29
1985	Asir, 5-11-7	P Kelleway	R Beggan	9/1	27
1986	Ten Plus, 6-11-7	F Walwyn	K Mooney	5/2f	28
1987	The West Awake, 6-11-7	O Sherwood	S Sherwood	16/1	28
1988	Rebel Song, 6-11-7	O Sherwood	S Sherwood	14/1	25
1989	Sayfar's Lad, 5-11-7	M Pipe	M Perrett	12/1	22
1990	Regal Ambition, 6-11-7	M Pipe	P Scudamore	3/1f	22
1991	Crystal Spirit, 4-10-12	I Balding	J Frost	2/1f	29
1992	Thetford Forest, 5-11-7	D Nicholson	R Dunwoody	7/1	27

Janneau Mersey Novices' Hurdle
(Grade 2, Aintree, early April)
for four yrs old and upwards which, at the start of the
current season, have not won a hurdle race
TWO MILES ABOUT FOUR FURLONGS

Weights: 4-y-o . . . . 10st 8lb; 5-y-o and up 11st 1lb
Fillies and mares allowed 5lb
Penalties, a winner of a hurdle race value £5000 . . . . .4lb
Of a hurdle race value £10000 . . . . .8lb

	Winner	Trainer	Jockey	SP	Ran
1988	Sir Blake, 7-11-5	D Elsworth	B Powell	2/1f	13
1989	Morley Street, 5-11-5	G Balding	J Frost	7/2	10
1990	Vazon Bay, 6-11-0	Mrs J Pitman	M Pitman	33/1	10
1991	Shannon Glen, 5-11-1	Mrs J Pitman	M Bowlby	8/1	9
1992	Coulton, 5-11-1	M W Easterby	G McCourt	9/1	12

Two-mile hurdles

As the three-mile category is to the steeplechasers, so the two-mile division is to the hurdlers: the pinnacle.

The second championship event, the Champion Hurdle, is one of the great races of the season and, with the Gold Cup, forms not only the foundation of the National Hunt Festival at Cheltenham but of the entire season. Where it has differed significantly from the Gold Cup, at least in recent years, is in its greater continuity. Not since L'Escargot in 1970 and 1971 has the Gold Cup been won by the same horse in successive years.

During the same period Bula ('71 and '72), Night Nurse ('76 and '77), Monksfield ('78 and '79), Sea Pigeon ('80 and '81) and See You Then ('85, '86 and '87) have completed consecutive victories. To that list might also be added Comedy Of Errors, who regained the title in 1975, having won it in 1973 and lost it in between to Lanzarote.

The Champion Hurdle is the undisputed magnet for the two-mile hurdlers. It invariably attracts the best competitors around and more often than not is won by a genuine champion.

The first of the championship races, the Christmas Hurdle at Kempton Park, has never quite exerted the same pull, although it has still drawn two recent Champion Hurdle winners. Dawn Run won the race in 1983 before her Cheltenham triumph, while Kribensis, a former Flat racer ideally suited by a level track on which to exploit his finishing speed, has taken the race twice, on the second occasion as a preface to winning the Champion Hurdle. Browne's Gazette might have made it three but, having won at Kempton Park, started so slowly at Cheltenham that he effectively forfeited all chance from the outset.

In addition to the championship races, the lead-up races – notably the Fighting Fifth, the Bula Hurdle and the Kingwell Hurdle – have generally attracted the top hurdlers. Although they have not recently enjoyed the same consistent magnetism as they did during the '70s, when between them they were regularly contested and won by the likes of Comedy Of Errors, Bird's Nest, Sea Pigeon and Lanzarote, that may be due in part to the unusual preparations enjoyed by several recent Champion Hurdle winners.

Morley Street and Beech Road both returned to hurdling after unsuccessful spells steeplechasing, while See You Then's fragile legs

The 1990 Champion Hurdle (Cheltenham 2m): Kribensis (right), Past Glories (centre) and Beech Road

demanded as light a campaign as possible. That was no less the case with the 1992 winner Royal Gait, who won on only his fourth run over hurdles after having his career interrupted by leg problems. The consolation race, the Scottish Champion Hurdle at Ayr, reverted in 1991 to a non-handicap after a lengthy spell as a handicap. The handicap format tended to intimidate the top hurdlers because of the amount of weight they would have to give away and, while the race was well contested, the return to being a non-handicap immediately produced a top-class winner in Granville Again.

Bellway Homes Fighting Fifth Hurdle
(Grade 2, Newcastle, mid-November)
for four yrs old and upwards
TWO MILES ABOUT HALF A FURLONG

Weights: 11st each
Fillies and mares allowed 5lb
Penalties, after September 1st, 1991, a winner of a weight-for-age hurdle race value £5000 . . . . .4lb
Of a weight-for-age hurdle race value £15000 . . . . .8lb

	Winner	Trainer	Jockey	SP	Ran
1987	Floyd, 7-11-6	D Elsworth	C Brown	5/6f	7
1988	Floyd, 8-11-6	D Elsworth	S Sherwood	9/4	6
1989	Kribensis, 5-11-9	M Stoute	M Dwyer	4/7f	5
1990	Beech Road, 8-11-4	G Balding	R Guest	4/6f	5
1991	Royal Derbi, 6-11-4	N Callaghan	C Grant	7/2	4

Arlington Bula Hurdle
(Grade 2, Cheltenham, early December)
for four yrs old and upwards
TWO MILES ABOUT ONE FURLONG

Weights: 11st each
Fillies and mares allowed 5lb
Penalties, after 1990, a winner of a weight-for-age hurdle race value
£4000 . . . . .4lb
Of a weight-for-age hurdle race value £10000 . . . . .8lb
Half penalties for horses which, before August 2nd, 1991, have not won
a hurdle race

	Winner	Trainer	Jockey	SP	Ran
1987	Pat's Jester, 4-11-2	R Allan	P Niven	11/2	8
1988	Condor Pan, 5-11-2	J Bolger (Ire)	C Swan	12/1	8
1989	Cruising Altitude, 6-11-4	O Sherwood	J Osborne	8/11f	8
1990	abandoned, snow				
1991	Royal Derbi, 6-11-8	N Callaghan	D J Murphy	9/2	5

Christmas Hurdle
(Grade 1, Kempton Park, late December)
for four yrs old and upwards
about TWO MILES

Weights: 11st 7lb each
Fillies and mares allowed 5lb

	Winner	Trainer	Jockey	SP	Ran
1982	Ekbalco, 6-11-13	R Fisher	J J O'Neill	1/2f	4
1983	Dawn Run, 5-10-12	P Mullins (Ire)	J J O'Neill	9/4	4
1984	Browne's Gazette, 6-11-3	Mrs M Dickinson	D Browne	11/8f	7
1985	Aonoch, 6-11-3	Mrs S Oliver	J Duggan	14/1	9
1986	Nohalmdun, 5-11-3	M H Easterby	P Scudamore	15/8f	7
1987	Osric, 4-11-3	M Ryan	G McCourt	12/1	8
1988	Kribensis, 4-11-3	M Stoute	R Dunwoody	4/9f	7
1989	Kribensis, 5-11-3	M Stoute	R Dunwoody	4/6f	7
1990	Fidway, 5-11-7	T Thomson Jones	S Smith Eccles	100/30	8
1991	Gran Alba, 5-11-7	R Hannon	G McCourt	3/1	7

Champion Hurdle Trial
(Grade 2, Haydock Park, late January)
for five yrs old and upwards
about TWO MILES

Weights: 11st 3lb each
Mares allowed 5lb
Penalties, after July 1st 1991, a winner of a weight-for-age hurdle race
value £4500 . . . . .4lb
Of a weight-for-age hurdle race value £10000 . . . . .7lb

	Winner	Trainer	Jockey	SP	Ran
1988	abandoned, snow				
1989	Vicario Di Bray, 6-11-8	J J O'Neill	M Dwyer	11/1	6
1990	Bank View, 5-11-8	N Tinkler	G Bradley	33/1	7
1991	abandoned, frost				
1992	Granville Again, 6-11-10	M Pipe	P Scudamore	1/2f	5

Kingwell Hurdle
(Grade 2, Wincanton, late February)
for four yrs old and upwards
about TWO MILES

Weights: 4-y-o . . . . 10st 6lb; 5-y-o and up 11st 2lb
Fillies and mares allowed 5lb
Penalties, after July 1st 1991, a winner of a weight-for-age hurdle race
value £6000 . . . . .5lb
Of a weight-for-age hurdle race value £12000 . . . . .8lb

	Winner	Trainer	Jockey	SP	Ran
1988	Floyd, 8-11-8	D Elsworth	C Brown	9/2	8
1989	Floyd, 9-11-8	D Elsworth	R Dunwoody	10/11f	5
1990	Kribensis, 6-11-12	M Stoute	R Dunwoody	4/6f	8
1991	Welsh Bard, 7-11-12	C Brooks	P Scudamore	11/1	7
1992	Fidway, 7-11-10	T Thomson Jones	P Scudamore	11/4	6

Smurfit Champion Hurdle Challenge Trophy
(Grade 1, Cheltenham, mid-March)
for four yrs old and upwards
TWO MILES ABOUT HALF A FURLONG

Weights: 4-y-o . . . . .11st 6lb; 5-y-o and up 12st
Fillies and mares allowed 5lb

	Winner	Trainer	Jockey	SP	Ran
1983	Gaye Brief, 6-12-0	Mrs M Rimell	R Linley	7/1	17
1984	Dawn Run, 6-11-9	P Mullins (Ire)	J J O'Neill	4/5f	14
1985	See You Then, 5-12-0	N Henderson	S Smith-Eccles	16/1	14
1986	See You Then, 6-12-0	N Henderson	S Smith-Eccles	5/6f	23
1987	See You Then, 7-12-0	N Henderson	S Smith-Eccles	11/10f	18
1988	Celtic Shot, 6-12-0	F Winter	P Scudamore	7/1	21
1989	Beech Road, 7-12-0	G Balding	R Guest	50/1	15
1990	Kribensis, 6-12-0	M Stoute	R Dunwoody	95/40	19
1991	Morley Street, 7-12-0	G Balding	J Frost	4/1f	24
1992	Royal Gait, 9-12-0	J Fanshawe	G McCourt	6/1	16

Scottish Champion Hurdle
(Grade 2, Ayr, mid-April)
for four yrs old and upwards
about TWO MILES

Weights: 4-y-o . . . . .10st 10lb; 5-y-o and up 11st 2lb
Fillies and mares allowed 5lb
Penalties, after 1990, a winner of a weight-for-age hurdle race value
£5000 . . . . .4lb
Of a weight-for-age hurdle race value £15000 . . . . .8lb

	Winner	Trainer	Jockey	SP	Ran
1988*	Pat's Jester, 5-11-1	R Allan	B Storey	5/1	8
1989*	Aldino, 6-12-0	O Sherwood	S Sherwood	13/2	6
1990*	Sayparee, 5-10-7	M Pipe	J Lower	11/2	13
1991	Precious Boy, 5-11-2	M O'Neill	L Wyer	9/2	5
1992	Granville Again, 6-11-10	M Pipe	P Scudamore	4/7f	5

* Run as a handicap before 1991

Two-and-a-half mile hurdles

Rather like its steeplechasing equivalent, the two-and-a-half mile hurdling division attracts an often floating population. Its races are contested by horses either moving up or coming down in distance: by two-milers being asked to take on another half-mile, or by stayers travelling in the opposite direction.

That principle holds good for most of the races in the category and is illustrated by the 1991 Racecall Ascot Hurdle, the first of the lead-up races. Morley Street, the 1991 Champion Hurdle winner, took on King's Curate, the leading stayer, and in a close finish Morley Street had the final word. This is the division where the opposite ends of the distance spectrum will most often meet.

The other three lead-up races in this still-developing category are still too young to display any obvious traits, but the consolation race, the St Modwen Staffordshire Hurdle at Uttoxeter, has produced one excellent talking point. Norton's Coin, the 1990 Cheltenham Gold Cup winner, made his hurdling debut at the age of 10 the following year but had to settle for second behind Randolph Place.

Curiously, there does seem to be a distinction between the two championship races, the Bishops Cleeve Hurdle at Cheltenham and the Martell Aintree Hurdle. The Cheltenham race, perhaps because of the testing nature of the course, has been the more natural home of the stayer. In the last ten runnings, Rose Ravine, Cloughtaney, Calapaez and Crystal Spirit have all been better served by longer rather than shorter trips.

The Martell Aintree Hurdle has, however, proved a more success-ful hunting ground for the primarily two-milers. Indeed, its position in the calendar has made it an obvious target for the Champion Hurdle winner after Cheltenham. There have been exceptions – Aonoch, a high-class stayer, won successive runnings in 1986 and 1987 – but the Champion Hurdle has proved a reliable guide to the race. Four of the last 10 renewals have gone to horses adding to a Champion Hurdle win, Gaye Brief, Dawn Run, Beech Road and in 1991 Morley Street, the second of his three consecutive victories.

The Martell has often been a magnificent contest, its position on the day's programme as the race before the Grand National tapping the rising tide of emotion. Morley Street's wins have oozed quality, but surely for pure excitement few races anywhere can have matched Night Nurse's thrilling dead-heat with Monksfield in 1977. Two brilliant horses, Night Nurse, the title holder but who was due to surrender the crown to Monksfield the following year, locked together, both giving everything. It was a spectacle which epitomised top-class racing and, although staged before the Pattern reached its present sophistication, captured its soul: great horses, great races.

Racecall Ascot Hurdle
(Grade 2, Ascot, mid-November)
for four yrs old and upwards
TWO MILES ABOUT FOUR FURLONGS

Weights: 11st each
Fillies and mares allowed 5lb
Penalties, after 1991, a winner of a weight-for-age hurdle race value
£5000 . . . . .5lb
Of a weight-for-age hurdle race value £15000 .10lb

	Winner	Trainer	Jockey	SP	Ran
1987	Sabin Du Loir, 8-10-11	M Pipe	P Scudamore	5/2	7
1988	Sabin Du Loir, 9-10-11	M Pipe	P Scudamore	1/2f	6
1989	Nodform, 5-10-11	J Gifford	R Rowe	12/1	5
1990	Morley Street, 6-11-10	G Balding	J Frost	4/5f	5
1991	Morley Street, 7-11-10	G Balding	J Frost	4/9f	6

Kilroe Group Waterloo Hurdle
(Grade 2, Haydock Park, mid-December)
for four yrs old and upwards
TWO MILES ABOUT FOUR FURLONGS

Weights: 11st each
Fillies and mares allowed 5lb
Penalties, after 1990, a winner of a weight-for-age hurdle race value
£4000 . . . . .4lb
Of a weight-for-age hurdle race value £10000 . . . . .8lb
(Half penalties for horses which, before August 2nd 1991, have not won
a hurdle race)

	Winner	Trainer	Jockey	SP	Ran
1990	Run For Free, 6-11-2	M Pipe	J Lower	11/1	9
1991	abandoned, frost				

Bishops Cleeve Hurdle
(Grade 1, Cheltenham, late January)
for four yrs old and upwards
TWO MILES ABOUT FIVE FURLONGS

Weights: 4-y-o . . . . 10st 9lb; 5-y-o and up 11st 8lb
Fillies and mares allowed 5lb

	Winner	Trainer	Jockey	SP	Ran
1983	Al Kuwait, 7-11-10	F Winter	J Francome	3/1	5
1984	Buckbe, 5-11-5	D Elsworth	C Brown	6/4f	10
1985	Rose Ravine, 6-11-5	F Walwyn	R Pusey	100/30	9
1986	Stans Pride, 9-11-5	G Price	R Beggan	17/2	8
1987	abandoned, frost				
1988	Cloughtaney, 7-12-0	P Mullins (Ire)	A Mullins	5/2jf	11
1989	Calapaez, 5-11-10	Miss B Sanders	S Sherwood	6/4	4
1990	Beech Road, 8-12-0	G Balding	R Guest	1/3f	5
1991	Crystal Spirit, 4-10-9	I Balding	J Frost	4/1	9
1992	abandoned, frost				

41

Regency Hurdle
(Grade 2, Warwick, mid-February)
for four yrs old and upwards
TWO MILES ABOUT FOUR AND A HALF FURLONGS

Weights: 4-y-o . . . . 10st 8lb; 5-y-o and up 11st 5lb
Fillies and mares allowed 5lb
Penalties a winner of a weight-for-age hurdle race value £5000 . . . . . .4lb
Of a weight-for-age hurdle race value £10000 .7lb

	Winner	Trainer	Jockey	SP	Ran
1991	Run For Free, 7-11-12	M Pipe	P Scudamore	6/5f	9
1992	Don Valentino, 7-11-5	Mrs J Pitman	M Pitman	33/1	10

Berkshire Hurdle
(Grade 2, Newbury, early March)
for four yrs old and upwards
TWO MILES ABOUT FIVE FURLONGS

Weights: 4-y-o . . . . .10st 10lb; 5-y-o and up 11st 5lb
Fillies and mares allowed 5lb
Penalties, a winner of a weight-for-age hurdle race value £5000 . . . . .4lb
Of a weight-for-age hurdle race value £10000 .7lb

	Winner	Trainer	Jockey	SP	Ran
1991	Morley Street, 7-11-12	G Balding	J Frost	8/11f	6
1992	Crystal Spirit, 5-11-12	I Balding	J Frost	11/10f	8

The 1992 Martell Aintree Hurdle (2½m): Morley Street leads Minorettes Girl

Martell Aintree Hurdle
(Grade 1, Aintree, early April)
for four yrs old and upwards
TWO MILES ABOUT FOUR FURLONGS

Weights: 4-y-o .... 11st; 5-y-o and up 11st 7lb
Fillies and mares allowed 5lb

	Winner	Trainer	Jockey	SP	Ran
1983	Gaye Brief, 6-11-11	Mrs M Rimell	R Linley	11/8f	6
1984	Dawn Run, 6-11-6	P Mullins (Ire)	A Mullins	4/6f	8
1985	Bajan Sunshine, 6-11-6	M Tate	P Scudamore	11/1	7
1986	Aonoch, 7-11-9	Mrs S Oliver	J Duggan	16/1	9
1987	Aonoch, 8-11-9	Mrs S Oliver	Jacqui Oliver	5/2f	7
1988	Celtic Chief, 5-11-6	Mrs M Rimell	R Dunwoody	4/5f	9
1989	Beech Road, 7-11-9	G Balding	R Guest	10/1	12
1990	Morley Street, 6-11-6	G Balding	J Frost	4/5f	6
1991	Morley Street, 7-11-7	G Balding	J Frost	11/8f	9
1992	Morley Street, 8-11-7	G Balding	R Dunwoody	4/5f	6

St Modwen Staffordshire Hurdle
(Grade 2, Uttoxeter, late April/early May)
for four yrs old and upwards
TWO MILES ABOUT FOUR AND A HALF FURLONGS

Weights: 4-y-o .... 10st 9lb; 5-y-o and up 11st 2lb
Fillies and mares allowed 5lb
Penalties, after 1990, a winner of a weight-for-age hurdle race value
£5000 .... 4lb
Of a weight-for-age hurdle race value £15000 .... 8lb

	Winner	Trainer	Jockey	SP	Ran
1991	Randolph Place, 10-11-2	G Richards	N Doughty	9/2	10
1992	Coulton, 5-11-6	M W Easterby	J Osborne	9/2	9

Three-mile hurdles

Taken alongside the two-mile hurdles, this division is further proof of continuity among the leading hurdlers. Although its performers do not quite measure up to the historical consistency found most markedly in the Champion Hurdle, they have still returned regularly enough to old haunts to acquit themselves well.

This is a division populated largely by proven stayers whose preferences will by this stage be well known. There is no better example than Galmoy. The fact that he was trained in Ireland by John Mulhern put him outside the boundaries of the Pattern for much of his career, but his record in the Stayers' Hurdle at Cheltenham left no doubt that at his best he was the pick of his contemporaries.

Twice he won, and his attempt at a third consecutive success was denied only by Rustle, who beat him into a meritorious second. Rustle was himself a good stayer, and might himself have added another Stayers' Hurdle to his record had not injury and a brief but unsuccessful flirtation with steeplechasing intervened.

Galmoy returned in each of the two following seasons but, by now a shadow of his top-class best, was unplaced on both occasions.

Trapper John was another good advertisement for the continuity theory. He won in 1990 and, after missing the race in 1991, returned in 1992 to finish second to Nomadic Way only to be disqualified because his rider failed to draw the correct weight. Trapper John, although like Galmoy trained in Ireland, has been a more regular visitor for the lead-up races. His trainer Mouse Morris was quick to take advantage of the newly-instituted Newbury Long Distance Hurdle in 1990 and Trapper John was also successful in the Premier Long Distance Hurdle at Haydock Park in 1992.

The introduction of the two early-season lead-up races, at Newbury and the West Yorkshire Hurdle at Wetherby, has proved an unqualified success. Apart from attracting Trapper John to Newbury, the races combined to promote an exciting recruit in Cab On Target, who won both races during the 1991-92 season. Unfortunately, he was denied the opportunity to be an even better ambassador for his trainer Mary Reveley, and indeed for the Pattern, when he was laid low by a virus while being prepared for the Stayers' Hurdle at Cheltenham.

The first of the championship races, the Long Walk Hurdle at Ascot, usually draws a sound, competitive field from the leading stayers, although curiously few recent winners have gone on to succeed at Cheltenham. Crimson Embers was an exception, despite a two season interval between his Ascot and Cheltenham wins. It should be said that Rustle might also have completed the double had he not fallen when in the lead at Ascot, the same season as his Cheltenham triumph.

West Yorkshire Hurdle
(Grade 2, Wetherby, early November)
for four yrs old and upwards
THREE MILES ABOUT ONE FURLONG

Weights: 4-y-o . . . . 10st 13lb; 5-y-o and up 11st
Fillies and mares allowed 5lb
Penalties, after 1990, a winner of a weight-for-age hurdle race value
£5000 . . . . .4lb
Of a weight-for-age hurdle race value £10000 . . . . .7lb

	Winner	Trainer	Jockey	SP	Ran
1990	Battalion, 6-11-7	C Brooks	P Scudamore	11/8f	10
1991	Cab On Target, 5-11-4	Mrs G Reveley	P Niven	5/2jf	6

Newbury Long Distance Hurdle
(Grade 2, Newbury, late November)
for four yrs old and upwards
THREE MILES ABOUT HALF A FURLONG

Weights: 4-y-o . . . . 10st 13lb; 5-y-o and up 11st
Fillies and mares allowed 5lb
Penalties, after 1990, a winner of a weight-for-age hurdle race value
£5000 . . . . .4lb
Of a weight-for-age hurdle race value £10000 . . . . .7lb

	Winner	Trainer	Jockey	SP	Ran
1990	Trapper John, 6-11-7	M Morris (Ire)	C Swan	10/11f	3
1991	Cab On Target, 5-11-4	Mrs G Reveley	P Niven	5/4f	11

Youngmans Long Walk Hurdle
(Grade 1, Ascot, mid-December)
for four yrs old and upwards
THREE MILES ABOUT ONE AND A HALF FURLONGS

Weights: 11st 7lb each
Fillies and mares allowed 5lb

	Winner	Trainer	Jockey	SP	Ran
1982	Mayotte, 7-10-11	R Holder	P Richards	15/8f	11
1983	Crimson Embers, 8-10-11	F Walwyn	S Shilston	14/1	11
1984	Kristenson, 7-10-8	R Fisher	M Williams	7/2	11
1985	Misty Dale, 7-10-8	Mrs J Pitman	P Tuck	9/4f	8
1986	Out Of The Gloom, 5-10-8	R Hollinshead	P Scudamore	4/1	5
1987	Bluff Cove, 5-10-8	R Hollinshead	R Dunwoody	14/1	10
1988	French Goblin, 5-11-1	J Gifford	Peter Hobbs	3/1	10
1989	Royal Athlete, 6-10-8	Mrs J Pitman	D Gallagher	33/1	11
1990	Floyd, 10-11-7	D Elsworth	G Bradley	10/1	8
1991	abandoned, frost				

Premier Long Distance Hurdle
(Grade 2, Haydock Park, late January)
for five yrs old and upwards
about THREE MILES

Weights: 11st 3lb each

Mares allowed 5lb
Penalties, after November 1st, 1991, a winner of a weight-for-age hurdle
race value £5000 . . . . .4lb
Of a weight-for-age hurdle race value £10000 . . . . .7lb

	Winner	Trainer	Jockey	SP	Ran
1988	abandoned, snow				
1989	Out Of The Gloom, 8-11-7	M Pipe	P Scudamore	3/1	10
1990	Mrs Muck, 9-11-2	N Twiston-Davies	G Bradley	13/8f	7
1991	abandoned, frost				
1992	Trapper John, 8-11-10	M Morris (Ire)	C Swan	13/8f	8

Rendlesham Hurdle
(Grade 2, Kempton Park, late February)
for four yrs old and upwards
about THREE MILES

Weights: 4-y-o . . . . 10st 7lb; 5-y-o and up 11st 5lb
Fillies and mares allowed 5lb
Penalties, after 1991, a winner of a weight-for-age hurdle race value
£5000 . . . . .4lb
Of a weight-for-age hurdle race value £10000 . . . . .7lb

	Winner	Trainer	Jockey	SP	Ran
1988	King's College Boy, 10-11-5	Mrs M Dickinson	G Bradley	15/8f	8
1989	Cliffalda, 6-11-9	J Edwards	T Morgan	11/4	5
1990	Old Dundalk, 6-11-3	D Murray Smith	M Bowlby	33/1	7
1991	Floyd, 11-11-12	D Elsworth	G Bradley	11/2	10
1992	Forest Sun, 7-11-5	G Balding	J Frost	6/1	6

The 1991 Bonusprint Stayers' Hurdle (Cheltenham 3m 2f): King's Curate (left) and Run For Free

Bonusprint Stayers' Hurdle
(Grade 1, Cheltenham, mid-March)
for four yrs old and upwards
THREE MILES ABOUT TWO FURLONGS

Weights: 4-y-o . . . . 11st; 5-y-o and up. 11st 10lb
Fillies and mares allowed 5lb

	Winner	Trainer	Jockey	SP	Ran
1983	A Kinsman, 7-11-12	J Brockbank	T G Dun	50/1	21
1984	Gaye Chance, 9-11-10	Mrs M Rimell	S Morshead	5/1	14
1985	Rose Ravine, 6-11-5	F Walwyn	R Pusey	5/1f	22
1986	Crimson Embers, 11-11-10	F Walwyn	S Shilston	12/1	19
1987	Galmoy, 8-11-10	J Mulhern (Ire)	T Carmody	9/2	14
1988	Galmoy, 9-11-10	J Mulhern (Ire)	T Carmody	2/1f	16
1989	Rustle, 7-11-10	N Henderson	M Bowlby	4/1	21
1990	Trapper John, 6-11-10	M Morris (Ire)	C Swan	15/2	22
1991	King's Curate, 7-11-10	S Mellor	M Perrett	5/2f	15
1992	Nomadic Way, 7-11-10	B Hills	J Osborne	15/2	17

Letheby & Christopher Long Distance Hurdle
(Grade 2, Ascot, early April)
for four yrs old and upwards
about THREE MILES

Weights: 4-y-o . . . . 10st 9lb; 5-y-o and up 11st 3lb
Fillies and mares allowed 5lb
Penalties, a winner of a weight-for-age hurdle race value £6000 . . . . .4lb
Of a weight-for-age hurdle race value £12000 .7lb

	Winner	Trainer	Jockey	SP	Ran
1988	Gaye Brief, 11-12-2	Mrs M Rimell	D Browne	14/1	6
1989	abandoned, snow				
1990	Battalion, 6-11-7	C Brooks	B de Haan	100/30	8
1991	Mole Board, 9-11-3	J Old	J Osborne	6/1	7
1992	Pragada, 9-11-3	M Pipe	P Scudamore	5/1	12

Two-mile novice chases

The two-mile novice chases demonstrate one of the clearest progressions in the Pattern. Throughout the series of lead-up races, and from the recently instituted first championship race, there is one clearly-defined objective: the Arkle Challenge Trophy Chase at the Cheltenham Festival. Never was it better illustrated than during the 1988-89 season. Of the four lead-up race winners, only Fred The Tread, successful in the Hurst Park Novices' Chase at Ascot, missed the Arkle.

The Dragon Master, the winner of the Henry VIII Novices' Chase at Sandown Park, Sabin Du Loir (PML Lightning Chase at Ascot) and Phoenix Gold (Nottinghamshire Novices' Chase at Nottingham) were in the Cheltenham line-up. On the big day all were upset, but by no less than Waterloo Boy. A 20/1 outsider that day, he subsequently revealed himself to be a consistently high-class two-mile chaser.

The progression was again evident during the 1991-92 season. Deep Sensation won the PML Lightning Chase and the Nottinghamshire Novices' Chase before finishing fourth to Young Pokey in the Arkle.

These examples illustrate one of the primary aims of the Pattern, that good horses should run against each other. The virtue of this division is that two-mile novice chasers, once their quality has been established, have little reason to venture into other distances.

Indeed, the status and value of the Arkle can work in reverse, drawing in horses who have been running over longer trips. That was true in 1991 when Remittance Man, having shown himself adept at two-and-a-half miles, tackled the two-mile specialist Uncle Ernie in an intriguing contest. Remittance Man won the day, overcoming the northern-trained challenger by six lengths. Similarly, Tinryland, second to Young Pokey in 1992, had earlier won the Galloway Braes Novices' Chase over two-and-a-half miles at Kempton Park.

The results of the Arkle demonstrate just how stern a test is the home of steeplechasing for a novice. Any number of big reputations have been dented there, not least Sabin Du Loir's in his year, although he bounced back to hold his own among the very best for several seasons.

The consolation race, the Sandeman Maghull Novices' Chase at Aintree, has proved a mixed blessing for contestants moving on from the Arkle. In the last five years Danish Flight, in 1988, has been the only winner to attempt the double, but he found Jim Thorpe too good for him. Feroda was unplaced at Cheltenham before winning at Aintree but neither Boutzdaroff nor Young Benz had run in the Arkle. The latter pair, incidentally, beat horses placed in the Arkle in Young Snugfit and Uncle Ernie respectively.

Hurst Park Novices' Chase
(Grade 2, Ascot, mid-November)
for five yrs old and upwards which, at the start of the
current season, have not won a steeple chase
about TWO MILES

Weights: 11st each

Mares allowed 5lb
Penalties, a winner of a steeple chase value £4000 . . . . 4lb
Of a steeple chase value £6000 . . . . 7lb

	Winner	Trainer	Jockey	SP	Ran
1987	Barnbrook Again, 6-11-8	D Elsworth	S Sherwood	5/6f	5
1988	Fred The Tread, 6-11-4	T Casey	R Dunwoody	8/1	5
1989	Young Snugfit, 5-11-8	O Sherwood	J Osborne	11/8f	5
1990	African Safari, 6-11-0	Mrs S Smith	R Stronge	7/2	3
1991	Poetic Gem, 6-11-0	Mrs S Smith	R Guest	4/1	4

Henry VIII Novices' Chase

(Grade 2, Sandown Park, early December)
for five yrs old and upwards which, at the start of the
current season, have not won a steeple chase
about TWO MILES

Weights: 11st each

Mares allowed 5lb
Penalties, a winner of a steeple chase value £4000 . . . . .4lb
Of a steeple chase value £6000 . . . . .7lb

	Winner	Trainer	Jockey	SP	Ran
1987	Ballyhane, 6-11-2	J Gifford	R Rowe	9/2	8
1988	The Dragon Master, 6-10-12	R Waley-Cohen	G Mernagh	100/1	7
1989	Deep Flash, 6-11-2	J Edwards	T Morgan	4/5f	5
1990	Acre Hill, 6-11-0	N Henderson	R Dunwoody	6/5f	5
1991	Peanuts Pet, 6-11-0	B McMahon	T Wall	5/1	6

Northumberland Gold Cup Novices' Chase

(Grade 1, Newcastle, late December)
for four yrs old and upwards which, at the start of the
current season, have not won a steeple chase
TWO MILES ABOUT HALF A FURLONG

Weights: 4-y-o . . . . .10st 10lb; 5-y-o and up 11st 7lb
Fillies and mares allowed 5lb

	Winner	Trainer	Jockey	SP	Ran
1990	Moment Of Truth, 6-11-7	P Monteith	L O'Hara	9/2	11
1991	Clay County, 6-11-7	R Allan	B Storey	6/4f	10

PML Lightning Novices' Chase
(Grade 2, Ascot, mid-January)
for five yrs old and upwards which, at the start of the
current season, have not won a steeple chase
about TWO MILES

Weights: 5-y-o . . . . 10st 8lb; 6-y-o and up 11st 4lb
Mares allowed 5lb
Penalties, a winner of a steeple chase value £5000 . . . . 4lb
Of a steeple chase value £10000 . . . . 8lb

	Winner	Trainer	Jockey	SP	Ran
1988	Saffron Lord, 6-11-5	J Gifford	R Rowe	100/30	6
1989	Sabin Du Loir, 10-11-5	M Pipe	P Scudamore	6/5f	4
1990	Cashew King, 7-11-5	B McMahon	T Wall	12/1	3
1991	Uncle Ernie, 6-11-8	J Fitzgerald	M Dwyer	2/1	6
1992	Deep Sensation, 7-11-4	J Gifford	D Murphy	7/4	4

Nottinghamshire Novices' Chase
(Grade 2, Nottingham, mid-February)
for five yrs old and upwards which, at the start of the
current season, have not won a steeple chase
about TWO MILES

Weights: 5-y-o . . . . 10st 10lb; 6-y-o and up 11st 5lb
Mares allowed 5lb
Penalties, a winner of a steeple chase value £5000 . . . . 4lb
Of a steeple chase value £10000 . . . . 7lb

	Winner	Trainer	Jockey	SP	Ran
1988	Danish Flight, 9-11-5	J Fitzgerald	M Dwyer	5/1	4
1989	Phoenix Gold, 9-11-5	J Fitzgerald	P Scudamore	15/8f	6
1990	Cashew King, 7-11-10	B McMahon	T Wall	7/4	6
1991	abandoned, snow				
1992	Deep Sensation, 7-11-12	J Gifford	D Murphy	13/8jf	5

The 1992 PML Lightning Novices' Chase (Ascot 2m): Deep Sensation (right) wins from Young Pokey

Waterford Castle Arkle Challenge Trophy Chase
(Grade 1, Cheltenham, mid-March)
for five yrs old and upwards which, at the start of the
current season, have not won a steeple chase
about TWO MILES

Weights: 5-y-o . . . . 11st; 6-y-o and up 11st 8lb
Mares allowed 5lb

	Winner	Trainer	Jockey	SP	Ran
1983	Ryeman, 6-11-8	M H Easterby	A Brown	16/1	16
1984	Bobsline, 8-11-8	F Flood (Ire)	F Berry	5/4f	8
1985	Boreen Prince, 8-11-8	A McNamara (Ire)	N Madden	15/2	16
1986	Oregon Trail, 6-11-8	S Christian	R Beggan	14/1	14
1987	Gala's Image, 7-11-8	Mrs M Rimell	R Linley	25/1	19
1988	Danish Flight, 9-11-8	J Fitzgerald	M Dwyer	11/2	12
1989	Waterloo Boy, 6-11-8	D Nicholson	R Dunwoody	20/1	14
1990	Comandante, 8-11-8	J Gifford	Peter Hobbs	9/2	14
1991	Remittance Man, 7-11-8	N Henderson	R Dunwoody	85/40f	14
1992	Young Pokey, 7-11-8	O Sherwood	J Osborne	4/1	11

Sandeman Maghull Novices' Chase
(Grade 2, Aintree, early April)
for five yrs old and upwards which, at the start of the
current season, have not won a steeple chase
about TWO MILES
(Over the Mildmay Course)

Weights: 5-y-o . . . . 10st 10lb; 6-y-o and up 11st 3lb
Mares allowed 5lb
Penalties, a winner of a steeple chase value £7000 . . . . .4lb
Of a steeple chase value £12000 . . . . .7lb

	Winner	Trainer	Jockey	SP	Ran
1988	Jim Thorpe, 7-11-8	G Richards	C Grant	11/4	7
1989	Feroda, 8-11-8	A Moore (Ire)	T Taaffe	13/8f	6
1990	Boutzdaroff, 8-11-1	J Fitzgerald	D Byrne	8/1	14
1991	Young Benz, 7-11-3	M H Easterby	L Wyer	13/2	10
1992	Cyphrate, 6-11-3	M Pipe	P Scudamore	8/1	11

Two-and-a-half mile novice chases

The two-and-a-half mile novice chase has been promoted to the forefront of the Pattern alongside its senior brother, the open chase category over the same distance. It grew from the same thinking, that the two-and-a-half mile horse should not be forced into running over distances which are not its best, and that the category should establish itself as a championship division in its own right rather than be a staging post for horses moving either up or down in distance.

The division has already featured some high-class steeplechasers. Look no further than Remittance Man, who won the Rovacabin Noel Novices' Chase at Ascot and the Galloway Braes Novices' Chase at Kempton Park during the 1990-91 season.

That said, the division's difficulty in retaining its stars was soon evident. Rather than continue through to Ayr for the second championship race, the Edinburgh Woollen Mill Future Champions Novices' Chase, Remittance Man's trainer, Nicky Henderson, opted to return to two miles for the Arkle Trophy at Cheltenham. Henderson took the same route the following year with Tinryland, who won the Galloway Braes before going on to contest the Arkle.

In comparing championship races, though, it should here be noted that the Future Champions Chase has been run over two-and-a-half miles only in 1991 and 1992. Judgement should, therefore, be reserved for the time being.

Earlier graduates of the races in this category include Bonanza Boy, who never quite reached the top but still developed into a formidable handicap chaser, and more especially Blazing Walker. Blazing Walker has proved an excellent ambassador for this relatively new division. He won the Dipper Novices' Chase at Newcastle in 1989, in the days when the race was run in November, and progressed to the two-and-a-half mile open chases in fine style when winning the Mumm Melling Chase at Aintree.

There is perhaps another star in the making. The 1992 Scilly Isles Novices' Chase at Sandown Park saw an excellent display by Bradbury Star, his sixth win in as many completed steeplechase

The 1992 Scilly Isles Novices' Chase (Sandown Park 2m 4f): Bradbury Star

58

starts. He was, however, lost to the division when, instead of waiting for the Future Champions Novices' Chase, he stepped up to three miles, finishing second to Miinnehoma in the Sun Alliance Chase at Cheltenham and winning the Mumm Mildmay Novices' Chase at Aintree.

The Godiva Kingmaker Novices' Chase at Warwick, the last Pattern race of the National Hunt season, has been won by Martin Pipe in both its runnings, Anti Matter's success being emulated by Milford Quay.

Rovacabin Noel Novices' Chase
(Grade 2, Ascot, mid-December)
for five yrs old and upwards which, at the start of the
current season, have not won a steeple chase
TWO MILES ABOUT THREE AND A HALF FURLONGS

Weights: 11st 3lb each

Mares allowed 5lb
Penalties, a winner of a steeple chase value £4000 . . . . .4lb
Of a steeple chase value £6000 . . . . .7lb

	Winner	Trainer	Jockey	SP	Ran
1987	Bonanza Boy, 6-11-8	P Hobbs	Peter Hobbs	6/4f	7
1988	Larchwood, 7-10-10	S Christian	K Mooney	7/2	8
1989	The Proclamation, 6-10-12	N Henderson	R Dunwoody	5/2	7
1990	Remittance Man, 6-11-7	N Henderson	R Dunwoody	2/1	5
1991	abandoned, frost				

Dipper Novices' Chase
(Grade 2, Newcastle, mid-January)
for five yrs old and upwards which, at the start of the
current season, have not won a steeple chase
TWO MILES ABOUT FOUR FURLONGS

Weights: 5-y-o . . . . 10st 8lb; 6-y-o and up 11st 5lb
Mares allowed 5lb
Penalties, a winner of a steeple chase value £5000 . . . . .4lb
Of a steeple chase value £10000 . . . . .7lb

	Winner	Trainer	Jockey	SP	Ran
1987	Jim Thorpe, 6-11-13	G Richards	P Tuck	15/8	6
1988	Cool Strike, 7-11-6	G Moore	B Storey	9/2	6
1989	Blazing Walker, 5-11-9	W A Stephenson	C Grant	8/11f	6
1991	Meritmoore, 8-11-5	G Moore	J Callaghan	11/8f	5
1992	Gale Again, 5-10-8	W A Stephenson	C Grant	7/2	6

Note: Run in late November before 1991

Scilly Isles Novices' Chase
(Grade 1, Sandown Park, early February)
for five yrs old and upwards which, at the start of the
current season, have not won a steeple chase
TWO MILES ABOUT FOUR AND A HALF FURLONGS

Weights: 5-y-o . . . . 10st 10lb; 6-y-o and up 11st 6lb
Mares allowed 5lb

	Winner	Trainer	Jockey	SP	Ran
1983	Kilbrittain Castle, 7-11-0	F Walwyn	W Smith	6/4f	5
1984	Norton Cross, 6-11-10	M H Easterby	A Brown	2/1	6
1985	Karenomore, 7-11-5	M H Easterby	J J O'Neill	9/4	5
1986	Berlin, 7-11-10	N Gaselee	D Browne	5/2	6
1987	First Bout, 6-11-5	N Henderson	S Smith Eccles	11/10f	6
1988	Yeoman Broker, 7-11-0	J Gifford	R Rowe	7/4	5
1989	The Bakewell Boy, 7-11-6	R Frost	J Frost	6/1	4
1990	abandoned, course waterlogged				
1991	Tildarg, 7-11-6	O Sherwood	J Osborne	11/2	6
1992	Bradbury Star, 7-11-6	J Gifford	D Murphy	6/5f	9

Note: Run over 2m 18yd before 1988

60

Mitsubishi Shogun Galloway Braes Novices' Chase

(Grade 2, Kempton Park, late February)
for five yrs old and upwards which, at the start of the
current season, have not won a steeple chase
TWO MILES ABOUT FOUR AND A HALF FURLONGS

Weights: 5-y-o .... 10st 7lb; 6-y-o and up 11st 3lb
Mares allowed 5lb
Penalties, a winner of a steeple chase value £5000................. 4lb
Of a steeple chase value £10000 .... 7lb

	Winner	Trainer	Jockey	SP	Ran
1988	Saffron Lord, 6-11-9	J Gifford	R Rowe	13/8	5
1989	Brookmount, 7-11-9	J Gifford	Peter Hobbs	2/1f	8
1990	Combermere, 6-11-4	R Frost	J Frost	4/7f	3
1991	Remittance Man, 7-11-7	N Henderson	R Dunwoody	100/30	8
1992	Tinryland, 8-11-3	N Henderson	J Osborne	15/8f	7

Northern Trust Opal Novices' Chase

(Grade 2, Lingfield Park, mid-March)
for five yrs old and upwards which, at the start of the
current season, have not won a steeple chase
TWO MILES ABOUT FOUR AND A HALF FURLONGS

Weights: 5-y-o .... 10st 8lb; 6-y-o and up 11st 3lb
Mares allowed 5lb
Penalties, a winner of a steeple chase value £5000................. 4lb
Of a steeple chase value £10000 .... 7lb

	Winner	Trainer	Jockey	SP	Ran
1988	The Luckpenny Man, 9-11-4	T Clay	M Perrett	50/1	8
1989	Macroom, 7-11-4	S Mellor	G Charles-Jones	9/4jf	7
1990	not run, due to construction of all-weather track				
1991	Laundryman, 8-11-3	S Mellor	M Perrett	2/13f	2
1992	Black Humour, 8-11-3	C Brooks	G Bradley	7/4f	7

61

Edinburgh Woollen Mill's Future Champion Novices' Chase

(Grade 1, Ayr, mid-April)
for five yrs old and upwards which, at the start of the
current season, have not won a steeple chase
TWO MILES ABOUT FOUR FURLONGS

Weights: 5-y-o . . . . .11st; 6-y-o and up 11st 8lb
Mares allowed 5lb

	Winner	Trainer	Jockey	SP	Ran
1983	Mountain Hays, 8-11-8	M H Easterby	A Brown	11/10f	5
1984	Noddy's Ryde, 7-11-11	G Richards	N Doughty	4/11f	8
1985	Buck House, 7-11-10	M Morris (Ire)	T Carmody	4/6f	10
1986	Amber Rambler, 7-11-3	H Wharton	S Youlden	5/1	5
1987	General Chandos, 6-11-3	Mrs S Bradburne	Mr J Bradburne	8/1	6
1988	Jim Thorpe, 7-11-10	G Richards	M Dwyer	9/4	6
1989	Southern Minstrel, 6-11-13	W A Stephenson	C Grant	5/4f	7
1990	Celtic Shot, 8-11-13	C Brooks	G McCourt	5/2jf	12
1991	High Knowl, 8-11-8	M Pipe	G McCourt	15/2	6
1992	The Illywhacker, 7-11-8	Mrs J Pitman	M Pitman	6/1	10

Note: Run over 2m before 1991

Godiva Kingmaker Novices' Chase

(Grade 2, Warwick, early May)
for five yrs old and upwards which, at the start of the
current season, have not won a steeple chase
about TWO MILES

Weights: 5-y-o . . . . .10st 10lb; 6-y-o and up 11st 3lb
Mares allowed 5lb
Penalties, a winner of a steeple chase value £7000 . . . . .4lb
Of a steeple chase value £12000 . . . . .7lb

	Winner	Trainer	Jockey	SP	Ran
1991	Anti Matter, 6-11-7	M Pipe	P Scudamore	8/11f	4
1992	Milford Quay, 9-11-7	M Pipe	P Scudamore	5/2f	7

Three-mile novice chases

To borrow, and slightly misquote, a footballing saying, this is effectively a category of two halves. The two championship races, the Feltham Chase at Kempton Park and the Sun Alliance Chase at Cheltenham, have developed very different characters.

The Feltham Chase has been marked by relatively small turn-outs – not once during the last ten years have the runners reached double figures – whereas the Sun Alliance has regularly drawn large and often ferociously competitive fields.

The results bear out the comparative difficulty of winning the two races. There is no escaping the fact that six favourites have won in the last ten runnings of the Feltham, while in the same period only four market leaders have collected the Sun Alliance. The Sun Alliance is an especially difficult race to win and, arguably, the toughest championship race in any category. Three miles around such an examination as Cheltenham is a tough test for a novice, ruthlessly exposing stamina failings or jumping inadequacies.

The early lead-up races have yet to establish themselves fully. The Aga Chase at Worcester has only just been increased in distance while the Lowndes Lambert December Novices' Chase at Lingfield Park has had an interrupted recent history, not least because of the laying of the all-weather track at the Surrey course. The Lingfield race has nonetheless produced two fine staying novices in Nick The Brief and Sparkling Flame.

The races in the second half of the season have become ever more closely linked. The Reynoldstown Chase at Ascot, the Sun Alliance and the Mumm Mildmay Chase at Aintree have created an appealing trio of opportunities, so much so that a financial bonus has been offered on performances in the three races.

In 1990 Royal Athlete won at Ascot and Aintree, his chance of completing a memorable treble dashed by a fall in the Sun Alliance. Victory at Cheltenham went to stable companion Garrison Savannah, who won the Gold Cup the following year.

The West Of Scotland Novices' Chase at Ayr has tended to have a place a little aside from the other races in the group because of its geographical position. Although it was run over two-and-a-half miles before 1991, the change has not materially affected the fact that its appeal is greatest to northern-trained horses.

The consolation race, the Mumm Mildmay Chase, has usually attracted competitive fields. Aside from Royal Athlete's win, Bradbury Star followed his second to Miinnehoma in the Sun Alliance by winning at Aintree.

Aga Worcester Novices' Chase
(Grade 2, Worcester, mid-November)
for five yrs old and upwards which, at the start of the
current season, have not won a steeple chase
TWO MILES ABOUT SEVEN FURLONGS

Weights: 5-y-o . . . . 10st 13lb; 6-y-o and up 11st 1lb
Mares allowed 5lb
Penalties, a winner of a steeple chase value £4000 . . . . 4lb
Of a steeple chase value £6000 . . . . 7lb

	Winner	Trainer	Jockey	SP	Ran
1987	City Entertainer, 6-10-12	C Postlethwaite	M Dwyer	11/8f	15
1988	Vicars Landing, 5-10-11	O Sherwood	C Cox	5/4f	10
1989	Lauderdale Lad, 7-10-12	J King	B Powell	11/2	10
1990	Killbanon, 8-11-1	C Trietline	S Earle	11/4	8
1991	Captain Dibble, 6-11-1	N Twiston-Davies	P Scudamore	4/6f	10

Note: Run over 2m 4f before 1990

Lowndes Lambert December Novices' Chase
(Grade 2, Lingfield Park, early December)
for five yrs old and upwards which, at the start of the
current season, have not won a steeple chase
about THREE MILES

Weights: 5-y-o . . . . 10st 13lb; 6-y-o and up 11st
Mares allowed 5lb
Penalties, a winner of a steeple chase value £4000 . . . . .4lb
Of a steeple chase value £7000 . . . . .7lb

	Winner	Trainer	Jockey	SP	Ran
1987	no corresponding race				
1988	Nick The Brief, 6-11-4	J Costello	T Costello	6/5f	10
1989	no corresponding race, due to construction of all-weather track				
1990	Sparkling Flame, 6-11-0	N Henderson	J White	6/1	6
1991	River Bounty, 5-10-13	J Upson	R Supple	9/2	3

Feltham Novices' Chase
(Grade 1, Kempton Park, late December)
for five yrs old and upwards which, at the start of the
current season, have not won a steeple chase
about THREE MILES

Weights: 11st 7lb each
Mares allowed 5lb

	Winner	Trainer	Jockey	SP	Ran
1982	Gallaher, 6-11-4	F Walwyn	W Smith	10/11f	5
1983	Duke Of Milan, 6-11-4	N Gaselee	P Scudamore	9/4	6
1984	Catch Phrase, 6-11-0	J Gifford	R Rowe	9/2	3
1985	Von Trappe, 8-11-4	M Oliver	R Dunwoody	13/8f	7
1986	Aherlow, 6-11-0	S Christian	R Beggan	13/8f	6
1987	Twin Oaks, 7-11-4	D Murray Smith	P Croucher	9/4	6
1988	Sir Blake, 7-11-4	D Elsworth	B Powell	8/11f	4
1989	French Goblin, 6-10-11	J Gifford	Peter Hobbs	15/8f	7
1990	Sparkling Flame, 6-11-7	N Henderson	R Dunwoody	7/2	7
1991	Mutare, 6-11-7	N Henderson	R Dunwoody	11/8f	9

The 1992 Sun Alliance Novices' Chase (Cheltenham 3m 1f): Miinnehoma (centre), the winner from Bradbury Star

West Of Scotland Novices' Chase

(Grade 2, Ayr, late January)
for five yrs old and upwards which, at the start of the
current season, have not won a steeple chase
THREE MILES ABOUT ONE FURLONG

Weights: 5-y-o . . . . 10st 7lb; 6-y-o and up 11st 5lb
Mares allowed 5lb
Penalties, a winner of a steeple chase value £5000 . . . . .4lb
Of a steeple chase value £10000 . . . . .7lb

	Winner	Trainer	Jockey	SP	Ran
1988	Randolph Place, 7-11-7	G Richards	P Tuck	13/8	7
1989	Southern Minstrel, 6-11-7	W A Stephenson	A Merrigan	7/2	3
1990	Carrick Hill Lad, 7-11-11	G Richards	N Doughty	11/10f	4
1991	Over The Deel, 5-10-7	W A Stephenson	Mr K Johnson	8/1	9
1992	Jodami, 7-11-5	P Beaumont	P A Farrell	11/8f	8

Note: Run over 2m 4f before 1991

Reynoldstown Novices' Chase

(Grade 2, Ascot, mid-February)
for five yrs old and upwards which, at the start of the
current season, have not won a steeple chase
THREE MILES ABOUT HALF A FURLONG

Weights: 5-y-o . . . . 10st 8lb; 6-y-o and up 11st 5lb
Mares allowed 5lb
Penalties, a winner of a steeple chase value £5000 . . . . .4lb
Of a steeple chase value £10000 . . . . .7lb

	Winner	Trainer	Jockey	SP	Ran
1988	Kissane, 7-11-8	J Edwards	T Morgan	4/1	6
1989	Vulgan Warrior, 8-11-8	S Christian	J Osborne	8/1	6
1990	Royal Athlete, 7-11-8	Mrs J Pitman	M Pitman	11/4	7
1991	abandoned, frost				
1992	Danny Harrold, 8-11-5	Mrs J Pitman	M Pitman	2/1	3

Sun Alliance Novices' Chase
(Grade 1, Cheltenham, mid-March)
for five yrs old and upwards which, at the start of the
current season, have not won a steeple chase
THREE MILES ABOUT ONE FURLONG

Weights: 5-y-o . . . . 10st 8lb; 6-y-o and up 11st 4lb
Mares allowed 5lb

	Winner	Trainer	Jockey	SP	Ran
1983	Canny Danny, 7-11-4	J Fitzgerald	N Madden	33/1	14
1984	A Kinsman, 8-11-4	J Brockbank	T G Dun	10/1	18
1985	Antarctic Bay, 8-11-4	P Hughes (Ire)	F Berry	6/4f	11
1986	Cross Master, 9-11-4	T Bill	R Crank	16/1	30
1987	Kildimo, 7-11-4	G Balding	G Bradley	13/2	18
1988	The West Awake, 7-11-4	O Sherwood	S Sherwood	11/4f	14
1989	Envopak Token, 8-11-4	J Gifford	Peter Hobbs	16/1	15
1990	Garrison Savannah, 7-11-4	Mrs J Pitman	B de Haan	12/1	9
1991	Rolling Ball, 8-11-4	M Pipe	P Scudamore	7/2f	20
1992	Miinnehoma, 9-11-4	M Pipe	P Scudamore	7/2f	18

Mumm Mildmay Novices' Chase
(Grade 2, Aintree, early April)
for five yrs old and upwards which, at the start of the
current season, have not won a steeple chase
THREE MILES ABOUT ONE FURLONG
(Over the Mildmay Course)

Weights: 5-y-o . . . . 10st 8lb; 6-y-o and up 11st 3lb
Mares allowed 5lb
Penalties, a winner of a steeple chase value £6000 . . . . .3lb
Of a steeple chase value £15000 . . . . .6lb

	Winner	Trainer	Jockey	SP	Ran
1988	Delius, 10-11-3	R Lee	B Dowling	9/1	13
1989	Swardean, 7-11-3	R Lee	B Dowling	16/1	13
1990	Royal Athlete, 7-11-9	Mrs J Pitman	M Pitman	5/2f	11
1991	Sparkling Flame, 7-11-9	N Henderson	R Dunwoody	4/1f	13
1992	Bradbury Star, 7-11-9	J Gifford	E Murphy	6/4f	7

Two-mile chases

When the first National Hunt Pattern came into being in 1969, the Queen Mother Champion Chase (then the National Hunt Two-Mile Champion Chase) was given the highest financial allocation of the nine chases in the Pattern. That early recognition of its importance in the National Hunt calendar has never been challenged, and it remains the supreme test of the two-mile chasers.

However, the long-standing dearth of two-mile chasers (owners and trainers are always keen to move their charges up in distance to the more glamorous staying chase territory of the Cheltenham Gold Cup) has produced a series of small fields throughout this category. This is reflected in the results of the Queen Mother Champion Chase. Winners often return to defend their title successfully, because there are usually few genuine challengers. The last ten years have produced only six individual winners, the latest of them Remittance Man.

Of the lead-up races, the Plymouth Gin Haldon Gold Cup at Exeter has developed into an attractive starting point for two-mile chasers. Pearlyman, the dual Champion Chase winner, began his campaign there in 1987, although the concession of 8lb to the talented Very Promising proved beyond him. Barnbrook Again, also a dual Champion winner, won the race in 1988 before going on to success at Cheltenham.

The first of the championship races, the Castleford Chase at Wetherby, became a non-handicap for the 1990-91 season, thus becoming the natural objective for the top two-mile chasers in the first half of the season. The race provides the first 'peak' for the two-milers, in line with the Pattern Committee's thinking. However, even in its handicap days it was won by two recent Champion Chase winners, Badsworth Boy and Pearlyman.

The two lead-up races in the second half of the season, the Victor Chandler Handicap Chase at Ascot and the Game Spirit Chase at Newbury, have, despite regularly being competitive contests, proved inconsistent in attracting the best two-milers. There have, however, been glorious exceptions, notably Desert Orchid rallying close to home to beat Panto Prince by a head in a pulsating race for the Victor Chandler in 1989 and Waterloo Boy's emphatic victory in a fine race for the Game Spirit in 1992. Indeed, Waterloo

69

Boy made excellent use of Pattern opportunities in 1992, adding the Tingle Creek Chase at Sandown, the Castleford Chase and the Victor Chandler to his Game Spirit victory.

The division's consolation race, the Martell Aintree Chase, has been marked by competitive fields, although in recent seasons only Pearlyman in 1988 has attempted to follow up a Cheltenham win at Aintree. But he found the task beyond him and finished seventh to Prideaux Boy.

Plymouth Gin Haldon Gold Cup Chase
(Grade 2, Exeter, early November)
for five yrs old and upwards
TWO MILES ABOUT ONE AND A HALF FURLONGS

Weights: 11st each

Mares allowed 5lb
Penalties, after February 1st, 1990, a winner of a weight-for-age steeple chase value £7000 . . . . .3lb
Of a weight-for-age steeple chase value £12000 . . . . .6lb
(Novice Steeple Chases not to count for penalties)

	Winner	Trainer	Jockey	SP	Ran
1987	Very Promising, 9-11-0	D Nicholson	R Dunwoody	7/2	5
1988	Barnbrook Again, 7-11-0	D Elsworth	S Sherwood	4/6f	4
1989	Panto Prince, 8-11-0	C Popham	B Powell	4/11f	5
1990	Sabin Du Loir, 11-11-0	M Pipe	P Scudamore	13/8	7
1991	Sabin Du Loir, 12-11-6	M Pipe	P Scudamore	5/4f	6

Mitsubishi Shogun Tingle Creek Limited Handicap Chase
(Grade 2, Sandown Park, early December)
for five yrs old and upwards
about TWO MILES

Lowest weight . . . . .10st 7lb; Highest weight 12st
Penalties, after November 28th, a winner of steeple chase value
£4000 . . . . .4lb
Of a steeple chase value £7000 . . . . .6lb
Half penalties for horses originally handicapped at or above 11st 7lb
No penalty to increase a horse's weight above 12st

	Winner	Trainer	Jockey	SP	Ran
1987	Long Engagement, 6-10-2	D Nicholson	R Dunwoody	3/1	5
1988	Desert Orchid 9-12-0	D Elsworth	S Sherwood	5/2	5
1989	Long Engagement, 8-10-0	D Nicholson	B Powell	9/2	4
1990	Young Snugfit, 6-10-7	O Sherwood	J Osborne	7/2	5
1991	Waterloo Boy, 8-11-13	D Nicholson	R Dunwoody	7/4f	6

Castleford Chase
(Grade 1, Wetherby, late December)
for five yrs old and upwards
about TWO MILES

Weights: 11st 10lb each
Mares allowed 5lb

	Winner	Trainer	Jockey	SP	Ran
1982	Little Bay, 7-10-8	G Richards	R Barry	9/2	6
1983	Badsworth Boy, 8-12-0	M Dickinson	G Bradley	10/11f	5
1984	Ryeman, 7-11-10	Mrs M Dickinson	G Bradley	5/2	5
1985	Our Fun, 8-10-11	J Gifford	R Rowe	9/4	4
1986	Little Bay, 11-11-7	G Richards	P Tuck	9/1	8
1987	Pearlyman, 8-12-7	J Edwards	T Morgan	evensf	5
1988	Midnight Count, 8-12-2	J Gifford	Peter Hobbs	15/8	4
1989	Ida's Delight, 10-10-7	J Charlton	B Storey	17/2	5
1990	Waterloo Boy, 7-11-10	D Nicholson	R Dunwoody	6/4	5
1991	Waterloo Boy, 8-11-10	D Nicholson	R Dunwoody	4/11f	4

Note: Run as a handicap before 1990

Victor Chandler Limited Handicap Chase
(Grade 2, Ascot, mid-January)
for five yrs old and upwards
about TWO MILES

Lowest weight . . . . .10st 4lb; Highest weight 12st
Penalties, after December 12th, a winner of a steeple chase 4lb
No penalties for horses originally handicapped at or above 11st 7lb

	Winner	Trainer	Jockey	SP	Ran
1988	abandoned, fog				
1989	Desert Orchid, 10-12-0	D Elsworth	S Sherwood	6/4f	7
1990	Meikleour, 11-10-0	J Fitzgerald	D Byrne	10/1	10
1991	Blitzkreig, 8-10-4	E O'Grady (Ire)	T Carmody	11/4	5
1992	Waterloo Boy, 9-11-10	D Nicholson	R Dunwoody	6/4f	5

Game Spirit Chase
(Grade 2, Newbury, mid-February)
for five yrs old and upwards
TWO MILES ABOUT ONE FURLONG

Weights: 5-y-o . . . . 10st 8lb; 6-y-o and up 11st 3lb
Mares allowed 5lb
Penalties, after 1991, a winner of a weight-for-age steeple chase value
£6000 . . . . .4lb
Of a weight-for-age hurdle race value £12000 .7lb

	Winner	Trainer	Jockey	SP	Ran
1988	Very Promising, 10-11-6	D Nicholson	R Dunwoody	5/4	5
1989	Mr Key, 8-10-7	D Murray Smith	S Sherwood	14/1	6
1990	Feroda, 9-11-12	A Moore (Ire)	T J Taaffe	10/11f	4
1991	abandoned, frost				
1992	Waterloo Boy, 9-11-10	D Nicholson	R Dunwoody	10/11f	6

Note: Run as a handicap before 1991

The 1992 Queen Mother Champion Chase (Cheltenham 2m): Remittance Man leads

Queen Mother Champion Chase
(Grade 1, Cheltenham, mid-March)
for five yrs old and upwards
about TWO MILES

Weights: 5-y-o . . . . 11st 6lb; 6-y-o and up 12st
Mares allowed 5lb

	Winner	Trainer	Jockey	SP	Ran
1983	Badsworth Boy, 8-12-0	M Dickinson	R Earnshaw	2/1	6
1984	Badsworth Boy, 9-12-0	M Dickinson	R Earnshaw	8/13f	10
1985	Badsworth Boy, 10-12-0	M Dickinson	R Earnshaw	11/8	5
1986	Buck House, 8-12-0	M Morris (Ire)	T Carmody	5/2	11
1987	Pearlyman, 8-12-0	J Edwards	P Scudamore	13/8f	8
1988	Pearlyman, 9-12-0	J Edwards	T Morgan	15/8f	8
1989	Barnbrook Again, 8-12-0	D Elsworth	S Sherwood	7/4f	8
1990	Barnbrook Again, 9-12-0	D Elsworth	H Davies	11/10f	9
1991	Katabatic, 8-12-0	A Turnell	S McNeill	9/1	7
1992	Remittance Man, 8-12-0	N Henderson	J Osborne	evensf	6

Martell Aintree Limited Handicap Chase
(Grade 2, Aintree, early April)
for five yrs old and upwards
about TWO MILES

Lowest weight . . . . 10st 7lb; Highest weight 12st
(No penalties after the publication of the weights)

	Winner	Trainer	Jockey	SP	Ran
1988	Prideaux Boy, 10-10-7	G Roach	A Webb	25/1	13
1989	Feroda, 8-10-7	A Moore (Ire)	T J Taaffe	9/1	9
1990	Nohalmdun, 9-10-7	M H Easterby	L Wyer	11/1	12
1991	Blitzkreig, 8-10-13	E O'Grady (Ire)	T Carmody	4/1f	11
1992	Katabatic, 9-12-0	A Turnell	S McNeill	6/5f	4

Two-and-a-half mile chases

The reasons for the introduction of two-and-a-half miles as a championship distance in its own right can be most clearly appreciated in this division.

There were two principal lines of thought in providing championship tests at this distance. First, that there should be opportunities for the best horses over every recognised distance. Second, what might be discounted as an in-between distance is, in fact, of considerable importance. The horse who is best suited by this trip no longer needs to be trained for a championship distance which does not do it justice.

While the two-and-a-half mile specialist now has a home, the category also provides opportunities for the versatile. Consider Sabin Du Loir. Although he has successfully plied his trade from two to three miles, he has made an immediate impact in this division. Over two seasons, 1990-91 and 1991-92, he collected four of the 14 races involved, no mean achievement. During 1990-91 he took the Newton Chase at Haydock Park, the first championship race, and the Cavalier Chase at Worcester, and might well have improved that record but for a fall when favourite in the Marston Moor Limited Handicap Chase at Wetherby. The following season he added the Desert Orchid South Western Pattern Chase at Wincanton and the Peterborough Chase at Huntingdon.

Desert Orchid, now with a race named after him, has prospered at this distance, as has another Cheltenham Gold Cup winner Norton's Coin, who has twice landed the consolation, the South Wales Showers Caradon Mira Chase, also at the Gloucestershire course.

Although the consolation race is at Cheltenham, the second championship race misses the Festival, taking place instead at Aintree. If early signs are reliable, that might not be such a disadvantage.

The infant division quickly claimed a spectacular discovery, namely Blazing Walker. His blistering victory in the Mumm Melling Chase in 1991 announced his arrival in the big time. Unfortunately, injury prevented his reappearing in 1992 but the fact that his name was almost always linked with the King George VI Chase and the Gold Cup reflects the dilemma of the two-and-a-half mile races. The temptation to step horses up in distance to the perceived jackpot of three-mile races can be overwhelming for owners and trainers alike. Thus, the challenge for this category will be to establish its own identity. The performances of two top-class performers might, however, be of assistance. Remittance Man, fresh from his win in the Queen Mother Champion Chase at Cheltenham, followed Blazing Walker on to the roll of honour for the Melling Chase, while Katabatic, after winning the Martell Aintree Handicap Chase, took the South Wales Showers Silver Trophy at Cheltenham.

Desert Orchid South-Western Chase
(Grade 2, Wincanton, late October)
for five yrs old and upwards
TWO MILES ABOUT FIVE FURLONGS

Weights: 5-y-o . . . . 10st 12lb; 6-y-o and up 11st
Mares allowed 5lb
Penalties, a winner of a weight-for-age steeple chase value £4000 . . . .4lb
Of a weight-for-age steeple chase value £7000 .8lb

	Winner	Trainer	Jockey	SP	Ran
1987	Desert Orchid, 8-11-8	D Elsworth	C Brown	1/7f	3
1988	Desert Orchid, 9-11-8	D Elsworth	S Sherwood	2/7f	5
1989	Panto Prince, 8-11-8	C Popham	B Powell	2/9f	6
1990	Panto Prince, 9-11-8	C Popham	B Powell	4/6f	3
1991	Sabin Du Loir, 12-11-8	M Pipe	P Scudamore	8/11f	7

Peterborough Chase

(Grade 2, Huntingdon, late November)
for five yrs old and upwards
TWO MILES ABOUT FOUR AND A HALF FURLONGS

Weights: 5-y-o .... 11st; 6-y-o and up 11st 1lb
Mares allowed 5lb
Penalties, after 1990, a winner of a weight-for-age steeple chase value
£10000 .... 4lb
Of a weight-for-age steeple chase value £15000 .... 8lb

	Winner	Trainer	Jockey	SP	Ran
1987	Very Promising, 9-11-9	D Nicholson	R Dunwoody	2/7f	3
1988	Townley Stone, 9-11-1	J Webber	G Mernagh	4/5f	3
1989	Clever Folly, 9-11-1	G Richards	N Doughty	5/4jf	4
1990	Pegwell Bay, 9-11-1	T Forster	J Railton	11/10f	5
1991	Sabin Du Loir, 12-11-9	M Pipe	P Scudamore	4/7f	4

Newton Chase

(Grade 1, Haydock Park, early January)
for five yrs old and upwards
TWO MILES ABOUT FOUR FURLONGS

Weights: 5-y-o .... 10st 13lb; 6-y-o and up 11st 10lb
Mares allowed 5lb

	Winner	Trainer	Jockey	SP	Ran
1991	Sabin Du Loir, 12-11-10	M Pipe	M Perrett	1/2f	4
1992	Pat's Jester, 9-11-10	G Richards	N Doughty	7/1	6

Marston Moor Limited Handicap Chase
(Grade 2, Wetherby, early February)
for five yrs old and upwards
TWO MILES ABOUT FIVE FURLONGS

Lowest weight .... 10st 7lb; Highest weight 12st
(No penalties after the publication of the weights)

	Winner	Trainer	Jockey	SP	Ran
1991	Katabatic, 8-11-3	A Turnell	S McNeill	4/1	8
1992	abandoned, frost				

Westminster-Motor Taxi Insurance Cavalier Chase
(Grade 2, Worcester, late February)
for five yrs old and upwards
TWO MILES ABOUT FOUR AND A HALF FURLONGS

Weights: 5-y-o .... 10st 7lb; 6-y-o and up 11st 3lb
Mares allowed 5lb
Penalties, after 1991, a winner of a weight-for-age steeple chase value
£6000 .... 4lb
Of a weight-for-age steeple chase value £12000 .... 7lb

	Winner	Trainer	Jockey	SP	Ran
1988	Beau Ranger, 10-11-4	M Pipe	M Perrett	5/4f	4
1989	Beau Ranger, 11-11-8	M Pipe	P Scudamore	40/85f	2
1990	abandoned, course waterlogged				
1991	Sabin Du Loir, 12-11-10	M Pipe	P Scudamore	4/6f	8
1992	Star's Delight, 10-11-3	M Pipe	P Scudamore	2/1	5

78

Mumm Melling Chase

(Grade 1, Aintree, early April)
for five yrs old and upwards
TWO MILES ABOUT FOUR FURLONGS

Weights: 5-y-o . . . . 11st 2lb; 6-y-o and up 11st 10lb
Mares allowed 5lb

	Winner	Trainer	Jockey	SP	Ran
1991	Blazing Walker, 7-11-10	W A Stephenson	C Grant	5/1	7
1992	Remittance Man, 8-11-10	N Henderson	R Dunwoody	4/9f	4

South Wales Showers Silver Trophy Chase

(Grade 2, Cheltenham, mid-April)
for five yrs old and upwards
TWO MILES ABOUT FIVE FURLONGS

Weights: 5-y-o . . . . 10st 6lb; 6-y-o and up 11st
Mares allowed 5lb
Penalties, after August 1st, 1991, a winner of a weight-for-age steeple
chase value £8000 . . . . .4lb
Or, after July 30th, 1992, a winner of a weight-for-age steeple chase
value £15000 . . . . .7lb

	Winner	Trainer	Jockey	SP	Ran
1988	Beau Ranger, 10-11-0	M Pipe	P Scudamore	11/10f	5
1989	Norton's Coin, 8-11-0	S Griffiths	R Dunwoody	20/1	8
1990	Barnbrook Again, 9-11-10	D Elsworth	H Davies	6/4f	5
1991	Norton's Coin, 10-11-4	S Griffiths	G McCourt	9/4	4
1992	Katabatic, 9-11-4	A Turnell	L Harvey	8/13f	4

Three-mile chases

The three-mile chase category is the glamour section of the National Hunt Pattern. In the King George VI Chase and Cheltenham Gold Cup it provides two of jumping's traditionally great contests, household names both. The roll-call of these races is a potted history of long-distance steeplechasing. In the recent past, Desert Orchid dominated the division with four victories in the King George and a single famous Cheltenham triumph.

Before Desert Orchid there were the two Lads, Burrough Hill Lad and Wayward Lad. Wayward Lad's three King George wins are now overshadowed by Desert Orchid but they remain a magnificent achievement in a race which is always hotly contested. Dividing his second and third wins was Burrough Hill Lad, who succeeded where Wayward Lad failed by completing the King George-Cheltenham Gold Cup double, although not in the same season.

What other memories the races have provided! Dawn Run's stirring victory as she became the only horse to have won both the Champion Hurdle and the Gold Cup, Norton's Coin's 100/1 shock win, Garrison Savannah and The Fellow fighting out a pulsating finish up the hill, and Nupsala reducing a packed Kempton crowd to silence.

The lead-up races make extensive use of handicaps and the Agfa Diamond Chase at Sandown Park in early February has proved particularly informative. Charter Party won the race en route to his Gold Cup triumph in 1988 and Desert Orchid, running over a track he loved, followed suit a year later.

In the first half of the season, the Rehearsal Limited Handicap Chase at Chepstow has in recent years produced several stars. Ten Plus won the race during the 1988-89 season and Martin Pipe used the Rehearsal for Carvill's Hill to announce his rehabilitation in 1991. Carvill's Hill would start the Gold Cup an even-money favourite only, in a controversial race, to blunder his chance away. While his dream faded, The Fellow would once more be edged out, this time by the outsider Cool Ground.

The first of the lead-up races, the Charlie Hall Chase at Wetherby, although not a handicap, was becoming largely the province of high-class handicappers until Celtic Shot's successive wins upgraded the quality of the winners.

The consolation race, the Martell Cup, has proved to be inconsistent in its appeal. Wayward Lad, thought to be in decline at the time, proved everyone wrong by winning the race in 1987, while Desert Orchid has both won it and fallen in it. Toby Tobias followed his second to Norton's Coin at Cheltenham by winning it. Kings Fountain, a faller in the Gold Cup, won in 1992, capitalising on the last-fence departure of Arctic Call.

Tetley Bitter Charlie Hall Chase
(Grade 2, Wetherby, early November)
for five yrs old and upwards
THREE MILES ABOUT HALF A FURLONG

Weights: 5-y-o . . . . 11st; 6-y-o and up 11st 2lb
Mares allowed 5lb
Penalties, after 1990, a winner of a weight-for-age steeple chase value £5000 . . . . .4lb
Of a weight-for-age steeple chase value £10000 . . . . .8lb
(Novice Steeple Chases not to count for penalties)

	Winner	Trainer	Jockey	SP	Ran
1987	Cybrandian, 9-11-2	M H Easterby	C Grant	7/4	4
1988	High Edge Grey, 7-11-2	K Oliver	T Reed	13/2	10
1989	Durham Edition, 11-11-2	W A Stephenson	A Merrigan	33/1	7
1990	Celtic Shot, 8-11-2	C Brooks	P Scudamore	7/4f	7
1991	Celtic Shot, 9-11-10	C Brooks	G Bradley	4/5f	6

The 1990 King George VI Chase (Kempton Park 3m): winner Desert Orchid

Rehearsal Limited Handicap Chase
(Grade 2, Chepstow, early December)
for five yrs old and upwards
about THREE MILES

Lowest weight . . . . 10st 7lb; Highest weight 12st
Penalties, after November 21st, a winner of a steeple chase 3lb

	Winner	Trainer	Jockey	SP	Ran
1987	Western Sunset, 11-11-4	T Forster	H Davies	evens	2
1988	Ten Plus, 8-10-12	F Walwyn	K Mooney	4/5f	5
1989	Bonanza Boy, 8-11-10	M Pipe	P Scudamore	4/1	6
1990	Boraceva, 7-10-7	G Balding	J Frost	9/2	6
1991	Carvill's Hill, 9-11-12	M Pipe	P Scudamore	7/4f	6

King George VI Chase
(Grade 1, Kempton Park, late December)
for five yrs old and upwards
about THREE MILES

Weights: 11st 10lb each
Mares allowed 5lb

	Winner	Trainer	Jockey	SP	Ran
1982	Wayward Lad, 7-11-10	M Dickinson	J Francome	7/2	6
1983	Wayward Lad, 8-11-10	M Dickinson	R Earnshaw	11/8f	5
1984	Burrough Hill Lad, 8-11-10	Mrs J Pitman	J Francome	1/2f	3
1985	Wayward Lad, 10-11-10	Mrs M Dickinson	G Bradley	12/1	5
1986	Desert Orchid, 7-11-10	D Elsworth	S Sherwood	16/1	9
1987	Nupsala, 8-11-10	F Doumen (Fr)	A Pommier	25/1	9
1988	Desert Orchid, 9-11-10	D Elsworth	S Sherwood	1/2f	5
1989	Desert Orchid, 10-11-10	D Elsworth	R Dunwoody	4/6f	6
1990	Desert Orchid, 11-11-10	D Elsworth	R Dunwoody	9/4f	9
1991	The Fellow, 6-11-10	F Doumen (Fr)	A Kondrat	10/1	8

Peter Marsh Limited Handicap Chase
(Grade 2, Haydock Park, late January)
for five yrs old and upwards
about THREE MILES

Lowest weight . . . . 10st 10lb; Highest weight 11st 10lb
(No penalties after the publication of the weights)

	Winner	Trainer	Jockey	SP	Ran
1988	abandoned, snow				
1989	Bishops Yarn, 10-10-12	G Balding	R Guest	13/2	4
1990	Nick The Brief, 8-10-9	J Upson	M Lynch	15/8f	6
1991	abandoned, frost				
1992	Twin Oaks, 12-11-10	G Richards	N Doughty	5/4f	8

Agfa Diamond Limited Handicap Chase
(Grade 2, Sandown Park, early February)
for five yrs old and upwards
THREE MILES ABOUT HALF A FURLONG

Lowest weight . . . . 10st 7lb; Highest weight 12st
(No penalties after the publication of the weights)

	Winner	Trainer	Jockey	SP	Ran
1988	Charter Party, 10-10-11	D Nicholson	R Dunwoody	100/30f	11
1989	Desert Orchid, 10-12-0	D Elsworth	S Sherwood	6/5f	4
1990	abandoned, course waterlogged				
1991	Desert Orchid, 12-12-0	D Elsworth	R Dunwoody	4/6f	4
1992	Espy, 9-10-7	C Brooks	G Bradley	11/1	9

84

Tote Cheltenham Gold Cup Chase
(Grade 1, Cheltenham, mid-March)
for five yrs old and upwards
THREE MILES ABOUT TWO AND A HALF FURLONGS

Weights: 5-y-o . . . . 11st 4lb; 6-y-o and up 12st
Mares allowed 5lb

	Winner	Trainer	Jockey	SP	Ran
1983	Bregawn, 9-12-0	M Dickinson	G Bradley	100/30f	11
1984	Burrough Hill Lad, 8-12-0	Mrs J Pitman	P Tuck	7/2	12
1985	Forgive 'N Forget 8-12-0	J Fitzgerald	M Dwyer	7/1	15
1986	Dawn Run, 8-11-9	P Mullins (Ire)	J J O'Neill	15/8f	11
1987	The Thinker, 9-12-0	W A Stephenson	R Lamb	13/2	12
1988	Charter Party, 10-12-0	D Nicholson	R Dunwoody	10/1	15
1989	Desert Orchid, 10-12-0	D Elsworth	S Sherwood	5/2f	13
1990	Norton's Coin, 9-12-0	S Griffiths	G McCourt	100/1	12
1991	Garrison Savannah, 8-12-0	Mrs J Pitman	M Pitman	16/1	14
1992	Cool Ground, 10-12-0	G Balding	A Maguire	25/1	8

Martell Cup Chase
(Grade 2, Aintree, early April)
for five yrs old and upwards
THREE MILES ABOUT ONE FURLONG
(Over the Mildmay Course)

Weights: 5-y-o . . . . 10st 10lb; 6-y-o and up 11st 5lb
Mares allowed 5lb
Penalties, after July 30th, 1992, a winner of a weight-for-age
steeple chase value £10000 . . . . .4lb
Of such a steeple chase value £25000 . . . . .8lb

	Winner	Trainer	Jockey	SP	Ran
1988	Desert Orchid, 9-11-5	D Elsworth	S Sherwood	3/1	4
1989	Yahoo, 8-11-5	J Edwards	T Morgan	5/1	8
1990	Toby Tobias, 8-11-9	Mrs J Pitman	M Pitman	evensf	5
1991	Aquilifer, 11-11-5	M Pipe	R Dunwoody	11/2	5
1992	Kings Fountain, 9-11-9	K Bailey	A Tory	11/4f	8

The handicaps

In addition to the 84 races which comprise the main body of the National Hunt Pattern, there are two further pieces in the jigsaw. Although handicaps are incorporated into several of the established categories, 14 further handicaps – eight steeplechases and six hurdles – have been awarded Grade 3 status as a recognition of their importance both to those professionally involved in racing and to the public at large.

The championship races are the true measure of a horse's ability but a high-class handicap, attracting plenty of betting interest, will always be a highlight. For proof, look no further than the Grand National. The winner is rarely in the same class as the Cheltenham Gold Cup winner, but no racing event in the calendar quickens the pulse in quite the same way.

The Hennessy Gold Cup at Newbury and the Whitbread Gold Cup at Sandown Park may not hold quite the same fascination for the non-committed racing public, but their respective records in attracting top-class fields speak for themselves. Indeed, Burrough Hill Lad's performance in winning the 1984 Hennessy has, according to the ratings of senior National Hunt handicapper Christopher Mordaunt, never been bettered by any steeplechaser since, Desert Orchid included. Desert Orchid, too, has had his moments in handicaps, not least when winning the 1988 Whitbread.

The handicap hurdles draw the top hurdlers with less frequency than the chases, but they are no less competitive for that. Each of the sextet provides a lively betting heat, which in turn helps foster widespread media coverage and attractive prize-money.

While drawing comparisons between the Flat and National Hunt Patterns is largely meaningless, there is one point worth remembering. Unlike the top-class Flat horses, the leading National Hunt performers do regularly run in handicaps and enrich such races by doing so. The handicap ratings given to the top National Hunt horses are, therefore, not simply an academic exercise. They reflect weights a runner might well carry in earnest.

The three remaining contests of the 101-race Pattern are included at Grade 2, but in no particular category. They are the Gerry Feilden Hurdle at Newbury, for those with Champion Hurdle aspirations, the H & T Walker Steeplechase at Ascot (designed as a stepping stone for potentially top-class horses before they take on more experienced performers), and the Heidsieck Dry Monopole Novices' Hurdle at Aintree, a late season objective for the leading three-mile novice hurdlers.

William Hill Handicap Hurdle
(Grade 3, Sandown Park, early December)
for four yrs old and upwards
TWO MILES ABOUT HALF A FURLONG

Lowest weight . . . . 10st; Highest weight 12st
Penalties, after November 7th, a winner of a hurdle race value
£5000 . . . . .4lb
Half penalties for horses originally handicapped at or above 11st 7lb
No penalty to increase a horse's weight above 12st

	Winner	Trainer	Jockey	SP	Ran
1987	Celtic Shot, 5-10-6	F Winter	P Scudamore	6/4f	12
1988	Corporal Clinger, 9-10-7	M Pipe	M Perrett	9/2	13
1989	Liadett, 4-10-0	M Pipe	J Lower	12/1	6
1990	Wonder Man, 5-10-12	Mrs J Pitman	M Pitman	11/4f	13
1991	Balasani, 5-10-0	M Pipe	M Perrett	7/1	20

Tote Jackpot Handicap Hurdle
(Grade 3, Sandown Park, early February)
for four yrs old and upwards
TWO MILES ABOUT SIX FURLONGS

Lowest weight .... 10st; Highest weight 12st
Penalties, after January 23rd, a winner of a hurdle race value
£6000 ....6lb
Half penalties for horses originally handicapped at or above 11st 8lb
No penalty to increase a horse's weight above 12st

	Winner	Trainer	Jockey	SP	Ran
1988	Hill-Street-Blues, 10-10-2	J Fox	S Moore	25/1	17
1989	Special Vintage, 9-10-12	J Fitzgerald	M Dwyer	20/1	15
1990	abandoned, course waterlogged				
1991	Rouyan, 5-10-0	R Simpson	W Morris	8/1	15
1992	Black Sapphire, 5-10-0	M Tompkins	B Powell	33/1	12

Tote Gold Trophy Handicap Hurdle
(Grade 3, Newbury, mid-February)
for four yrs old and upwards
TWO MILES ABOUT HALF A FURLONG

Penalties, after January 30th, a winner of a hurdle race value
£10000 ....7lb

	Winner	Trainer	Jockey	SP	Ran
1988	Jamesmead, 7-10-0	D Elsworth	B Powell	11/1	19
1989	Grey Salute, 6-11-5	J Jenkins	R Dunwoody	8/1	10
1990	Deep Sensation, 5-11-3	J Gifford	R Rowe	7/1	17
1991	abandoned, frost				
1992	Rodeo Star, 6-10-10	N Tinkler	G McCourt	15/2	15

County Handicap Hurdle
(Grade 3, Cheltenham, mid-March)
for five yrs old and upwards which, before February
14th, have been placed first, second or third in a
hurdle race
TWO MILES ABOUT ONE FURLONG

Penalties, after February 27th, a winner of a hurdle race value
£5000 . . . . .7lb

	Winner	Trainer	Jockey	SP	Ran
1988	Cashew King, 5-10-4	B McMahon	T Wall	9/1	24
1989	Willsford, 6-10-8	Mrs J Pitman	M Bowlby	11/1	21
1990	Moody Man, 5-11-2	P Hobbs	Peter Hobbs	9/1	20
1991	Winnie The Witch, 7-9-8	K Bridgwater	D Bridgwater (7)	33/1	26
1992	Dusty Miller, 5-10-6	S Sherwood	J Osborne	9/1	27

EBF 'National Hunt' Novices' Handicap Hurdle
(Grade 3, Cheltenham, mid-April)
for novice five, six and seven yrs old only which,
before April 11th, have been placed first, second,
third or fourth in a E.B.F. Novices' Hurdle Qualifying
Race during the current season (Horses which have
won a hurdle race before the start of the current
season are not qualified)
TWO MILES ABOUT ONE FURLONG

Penalties, after April 10th, a winner of a hurdle race value £3500 . . . .5lb

	Winner	Trainer	Jockey	SP	Ran
1988	Western Dandy, 5-9-7	N Gaselee	N Adams (7)	33/1	24
1989	For The Grain, 5-11-10	J S Wilson	L Wyer	14/1	18
1990	Vazon Bay, 6-12-0	Mrs J Pitman	M Pitman	7/1	12
1991	Poetic Gem, 6-10-0	G Balding	R Guest	9/2	8
1992	Current Express, 5-12-0	N Henderson	R Dunwoody	6/1	13

Swinton Handicap Hurdle
(Grade 3, Haydock Park, early May)
for four yrs old and upwards
about TWO MILES

Lowest weight . . . . 10st; Highest weight 12st
Penalties, after April 24th, a winner of a hurdle race value £4000 . . . .6lb
Half penalties for horses originally handicapped at or above 11st
No penalty to increase a horse's weight above .12st

	Winner	Trainer	Jockey	SP	Ran
1988	Past Glories, 5-11-9	W Elsey	P A Farrell (4)	16/1	23
1989	State Jester, 6-10-0	W Elsey	J Quinn	14/1	18
1990	Sybillin, 4-10-1	J Fitzgerald	D Byrne	8/1	14
1991	Winnie The Witch, 7-10-2	K Bridgwater	D Bridgwater (5)	8/1	12
1992	Bitofabanter, 5-11-1	A Moore (Ire)	T Taaffe	14/1	22

Mackeson Gold Cup Handicap Chase
(Grade 3, Cheltenham, mid-November)
for five yrs old and upwards
TWO MILES ABOUT FOUR AND A HALF FURLONGS

Penalties, after October 31st, a winner of a steeple chase value £4000 3lb
Of a steeple chase value £6000 . . . . .6lb
No penalty to increase a horse's weight above .12st

	Winner	Trainer	Jockey	SP	Ran
1987	Beau Ranger, 9-10-2	M Pipe	M Perrett	13/2	14
1988	Pegwell Bay, 7-11-2	T Forster	P Scudamore	6/1	13
1989	Joint Sovereignty, 9-10-4	P Hobbs	G McCourt	10/1	15
1990	Multum In Parvo, 7-10-2	J Edwards	N Williamson	12/1	13
1991	Another Coral, 8-10-1	D Nicholson	R Dunwoody	15/2	15

Hennessy Gold Cup Handicap Chase
(Grade 3, Newbury, late November)
for five yrs old and upwards
THREE MILES ABOUT TWO AND A HALF FURLONGS

Penalties, after October 31st, a winner of a steeple chase value
£10000 . . . . .4lb

	Winner	Trainer	Jockey	SP	Ran
1987	Playschool, 9-10-8	D Barons	P Nicholls	6/1	12
1988	Strands Of Gold, 9-10-0	M Pipe	P Scudamore	10/1	12
1989	Ghofar, 6-10-2	D Elsworth	H Davies	5/1	8
1990	Arctic Call, 7-11-0	O Sherwood	J Osborne	5/1	13
1991	Chatam, 7-10-6	M Pipe	P Scudamore	10/1	15

Coral Welsh National Handicap Chase
(Grade 3, Chepstow, late December)
for five yrs old and upwards
THREE MILES ABOUT FIVE AND A HALF FURLONGS

Penalties, after November 28th, a winner of a steeple chase value
£5000 . . . . .4lb
Of 2 such steeple chases. 8lb
Half penalties for horses originally handicapped at or above 11st 7lb

	Winner	Trainer	Jockey	SP	Ran
1987	Playschool, 9-10-11	D Barons	P Nicholls	5/1	13
1988	Bonanza Boy, 7-10-1	M Pipe	P Scudamore	9/4f	12
1989	Bonanza Boy, 8-11-11	M Pipe	P Scudamore	15/8f	12
1990	Cool Ground, 8-10-0	R Akehurst	L Harvey	9/2	14
1991	Carvill's Hill, 9-11-12	M Pipe	P Scudamore	9/4f	17

AF Budge Gold Cup Handicap Chase
(Grade 3, Cheltenham, mid-December)
for five yrs old and upwards
TWO MILES ABOUT FIVE FURLONGS

Penalties, after November 28th, a winner of a steeple chase value
£4000 . . . . .4lb
Of a steeple chase value £6000 . . . . .6lb
No penalty to increase a horse's weight above 12st

	Winner	Trainer	Jockey	SP	Ran
1987	Bishops Yarn, 8-10-7	G Balding	R Guest	100/30	5
1988	Pegwell Bay, 7-10-13	T Forster	B Powell	7/2	10
1989	Clever Folly, 9-10-4	G Richards	N Doughty	4/1	6
1990	abandoned, snow				
1991	Kings Fountain, 8-11-10	K Bailey	A Tory	7/4f	8

Racing Post Handicap Chase
(Grade 3, Kempton Park, late February)
for five yrs old and upwards
about THREE MILES

Penalties, after January 30th, a winner of a steeple chase value
£10000 . . . . .3lb
No penalty to increase a horse's weight above 12st

	Winner	Trainer	Jockey	SP	Ran
1988	Rhyme 'N' Reason, 9-10-11	D Elsworth	B Powell	7/2f	12
1989	Bonanza Boy, 8-11-1	M Pipe	P Scudamore	5/1	11
1990	Desert Orchid, 11-12-3	D Elsworth	R Dunwoody	8/11f	8
1991	Docklands Express, 9-10-7	K Bailey	A Tory	7/2	9
1992	Docklands Express, 10-11-10	K Bailey	A Tory	6/1	11

Martell Grand National Handicap Chase
(Grade 3, Aintree, early April)
for seven yrs old and upwards – Rated 105 plus.
Unrated horses will not be qualified unless, before
February 7th, they have run three times collectively
in Steeple Chases or Hurdle Races in Great Britain
or in Ireland, or have won a Steeple Chase or Hurdle
Race in Great Britain or in Ireland, and provided that
the Handicapper is prepared to allot them a Rating
of 105 or more. In addition, horses which have been
placed first, second or third in either the Maryland
Hunt Cup, the Grand Steeple Chase de Paris or the
Velka Pardubicka will also be qualified, whether or
not the Handicapper can allot a rating
FOUR MILES ABOUT FOUR FURLONGS
(The Grand National Course)

(No penalties after the publication of the weights)
To be ridden either by:-
(a) Jockeys or Amateur Riders who have ridden not less than 15 winners
in steeple chases or hurdle races under the Rules of Racing and/or the
Rules of the Irish National Hunt Steeple Chase Committee before March
29th, 1993, or (b) subject to the approval of the Stewards of the Jockey
Club. Jockeys or Amateur Riders licensed or permitted by Turf Author-
ities other than the Jockey Club or the Irish National Hunt Steeple Chase
Commitee and who ride under the provisions of Rule 61 of the Rules of
Racing, or (c) subject to the approval of the Stewards of the Jockey Club,
Jockeys or Amateur Riders licensed or permitted by the Jockey Club or
the Irish National Hunt Steeple Chase Committee, who have ridden less
than 15 winners in steeple chases and hurdle races under the Rules of
Racing and/or the Rules of the Irish National Hunt Steeple Chase
Committee. Application forms for approval under (b) and (c) above will
be available from the Jockey Club Registry Office and must be completed
and submitted no later than March 19th, 1993

	Winner	Trainer	Jockey	SP	Ran
1988	Rhyme 'N' Reason, 9-11-0	D Elsworth	B Powell	10/1	40
1989	Little Polveir, 12-10-3	G Balding	J Frost	28/1	40
1990	Mr Frisk, 11-10-6	K Bailey	M Armytage	16/1	38
1991	Seagram, 11-10-6	D Barons	N Hawke	12/1	40
1992	Party Politics, 8-10-7	N Gaselee	C Llewellyn	14/1	40

William Hill Scottish National Handicap Chase
(Grade 3, Ayr, mid-April)
for five yrs old and upwards
FOUR MILES ABOUT ONE FURLONG

(No penalties after the publication of the weights)

	Winner	Trainer	Jockey	SP	Ran
1988	Mighty Mark, 9-10-5	F Walton	B Storey	9/1	17
1989	Roll-A-Joint, 11-10-0	C Popham	B Powell	4/1	11
1990	Four Trix, 9-10-0	G Richards	D Byrne	25/1	28
1991	Killone Abbey, 8-10-0	W A Stephenson	C Grant	40/1	18
1992	Captain Dibble, 7-11-0	N Twiston-Davies	P Scudamore	9/1	21

Whitbread Gold Cup Handicap Chase
(Grade 3, Sandown Park, late April)
for five yrs old and upwards
THREE MILES ABOUT FIVE AND A HALF FURLONGS

Lowest weight. . . . . .10st; Highest weight not to exceed. 12st
(No penalties after the publication of the weights)

	Winner	Trainer	Jockey	SP	Ran
1988	Desert Orchid, 9-11-11	D Elsworth	S Sherwood	6/1	12
1989	Brown Windsor, 7-10-0	N Henderson	M Bowlby	12/1	18
1990	Mr Frisk, 11-10-5	K Bailey	M Armytage	9/2f	13
1991	Docklands Express, 9-10-3	K Bailey	A Tory	4/1jf	10
1992	Topsham Bay, 9-10-1	D Barons	H Davies	9/2	11

Gerry Feilden Hurdle

(Grade 2, Newbury, late November)
for four yrs old and upwards which, before August
2nd, 1991, had not won a hurdle race
TWO MILES ABOUT HALF A FURLONG

Weights: 11st each

Fillies and mares allowed 5lb
Penalties, a winner of a weight-for-age hurdle race value £5000 . . . . .3lb
Of a weight-for-age hurdle race value £10000 . . . . .6lb

	Winner	Trainer	Jockey	SP	Ran
1987	Celtic Chief, 4-11-0	Mrs M Rimell	P Scudamore	8/11f	9
1988	Kribensis, 4-11-6	M Stoute	R Dunwoody	8/11f	5
1989	Cruising Altitude, 6-11-3	O Sherwood	J Osborne	6/5f	8
1990	Fidway, 5-11-6	T Thomson Jones	S Smith Eccles	7/2	5
1991	Gran Alba, 5-11-0	R Hannon	G McCourt	5/4f	6

H & T Walker Limited Handicap Chase

(Grade 2, Ascot, mid-November)
for five yrs old and upwards which, before August
2nd, 1991, had not won a steeple chase
TWO MILES ABOUT THREE AND A HALF FURLONGS

Lowest weight . . . . .10st 7lb; Highest weight 12st
Penalties, after November 7th, a winner of a steeple chase value
£5000 . . . . .4lb
No penalty to increase a horse's weight above 12st

	Winner	Trainer	Jockey	SP	Ran
1987	Weather The Storm, 7-11-10	A Moore (Ire)	T Taaffe	6/1	11
1988	Saffron Lord, 6-11-3	J Gifford	R Rowe	8/11f	5
1989	Man O'Magic, 8-11-5	K Bailey	M Perrett	9/1	11
1990	Blazing Walker, 6-11-6	W A Stephenson	C Grant	7/2	5
1991	Kings Fountain, 8-11-1	K Bailey	A Tory	7/2	8

Belle Epoque Sefton Novices' Hurdle
(Grade 2, Aintree, early April)
for four yrs old and upwards which, at the start of the
current season, have not won a hurdle race
THREE MILES ABOUT HALF A FURLONG

Weights: 4-y-o . . . . 10st 10lb; 5-y-o and up 11st 4lb
Fillies and mares allowed 5lb
Penalties, a winner of a hurdle race value £3500 . . . . .3lb
Of a hurdle race value £6500 . . . . .6lb

	Winner	Trainer	Jockey	SP	Ran
1988	Rustle, 6-11-7	N Henderson	M Bowlby	13/8f	12
1989	Boreen Belle, 7-11-2	W Harney (Ire)	C Swan	10/1	14
1990	Dwadme, 5-11-4	O Sherwood	J Osborne	5/1	10
1991	Derring Valley, 6-11-4	A Jones	G McCourt	25/1	16
1992	Barton Bank, 6-11-4	D Nicholson	C Llewellyn	20/1	15